TRANSNATIONAL BUSINESS AND CORPORATE CULTURE

PROBLEMS AND OPPORTUNITIES

edited by

STUART BRUCHEY
ALLAN NEVINS PROFESSOR EMERITUS
COLUMBIA UNIVERSITY

A GARLAND SERIES

GLOBAL EXECUTIVE INFORMATION SYSTEMS

KEY ISSUES AND TRENDS

ANIL KUMAR

GARLAND PUBLISHING, INC.
A MEMBER OF THE TAYLOR & FRANCIS GROUP
NEW YORK & LONDON / 2000

658,403
K96g

Published in 2000 by
Garland Publishing Inc.
A Member of the Taylor & Francis Group
19 Union Square West
New York, NY 10003

10 9 8 7 6 5 4 3 2 1

Library of Congress Cataloging-in-Publication Data

Library of Congress Cataloging-in-Publication Data is available from the
Library of Congress.

Printed on acid-free, 250-year-life paper
Manufactured in the United States of America

This book is dedicated with love to my parents, Sarla Kanwar and Jiwen Chander Kanwar for their inspiration and encouragement.

Contents

Preface

Information technology, if used effectively, can play a very important role in collecting, organizing, and presenting information to executives for decision making. Executive information systems (EIS) that became popular during the 1980s were developed to serve the information needs of executives. The demand for these systems led several vendors such as Comshare Inc. (Commander EIS), Pilot Software (Command Center), SAS Institute Inc. (The SAS System) and IBM Corp. (Executive Decisions) to develop off-the-shelf software. These software products provided relevant and timely information to executives for decision making. However, the executive information systems that were developed and used by organizations focused on the domestic environment.

The globalization of businesses and the merging of computers and communications technology transformed the way in which organizations operate. As a result of these changes it became pertinent that executives assess organizational opportunities and threats in the global arena. Lack of familiarity with foreign environments increased the need for information, which is global in scope. Prior research in the information systems area has focussed on developing systems for executives in domestic organizations. Very few studies have investigated the issues that are raised for developing systems for executives operating in global organizations. This research reports on a study conducted to identify and validate the key issues for designing, developing, using and managing a global executive information system (Global EIS). The study was conducted in three phases and results from all the phases are reported and analyzed.

The research study begins with an introduction of the globalization phenomenon and looks at the impact of globalization on executive decision making. In chapter I information systems (EIS) used by executives in corporations are examined and their unique capabilities discussed. The few studies that address the topic of global executive information systems are also examined. In chapter II a research framework for the study of global EIS is proposed. The individual variables and their interactions are identified and described. In the following chapters the results are discussed. In organizing this research I have tried to present the theory and practice of using information technology for executive decision making in global organizations. I strongly believe in the usefulness of developing global executive information systems and feel that we will see tremendous growth in this discipline in the future.

Acknowledgments

I am deeply indebted to Dr. Prashant P. Palvia at the University of Memphis for his guidance and encouragement. I would also like to express my appreciation for Dr. Ben Kedia at the University of Memphis, who provided valuable ideas and recommendations for this study. This research was made possible by financial assistance from the Wang Center for International Business at the University of Memphis. Finally, I would like to thank the members of my family: my wife Poonam, my son Anish and my daughter Sannah for their love and patience and my brother Sheikhar for his support.

Introduction

The phenomenon of globalization, which has dominated the 90s, has its roots in the 19th century. Even though we can trace back the origin of international trade to earlier centuries, for example the silk route, it was in the 19th century that trade was truly global in nature and scope. England and France, two of the major world powers of the 19th century were the leaders of trade during this period. The establishment of the East India Company by the British in India for trade purposes is an example. The East India Company that began with the trading of spices evolved over the years into the transfer of raw materials from India for manufacturing products in the UK. This provided a major boost to manufacturing industries in England. The finished products from these industries were then transported back to India for sale at higher prices. Both England and France invested hugely in the developing countries at that time, namely United States, Canada and Australia. Restrictions on trade, such as, flow of capital, manpower, trade barriers etc. were limited and trade flourished.

The early 20th century witnessed a period of slowdown. England and France were no longer the dominant powers in the world. Most of their colonies were achieving independence. The end of World War II saw the emergence of the new power centers in the world, like the United States. In the following years Japan recovering from the devastation of the war also emerged as a major economic power. Japan focused on exports, dominating in the automobile and electronics industries, to revive their economy. International trade was making a comeback. The trend of globalization in the last couple of decades was witnessing a revival.

The 90s are considered by many to be the decade in which globalization exploded. Vitalari and Wetherbe (as cited in Palvia, Palvia, & Roche, 1996) point out that organizations are going global to exploit global markets and gain competitive advantages. There is a visible shift in economic dynamics from the national economy to the world economy. The process of globalization is accelerating at a phenomenal rate and several major economic and political factors are responsible for triggering this phenomenon in recent years. The establishment of a single European market in 1992; *perestroika* and the breaking up of communism in Soviet Union and eastern Europe; the North American free-trade zone consisting of the United States, Canada, and Mexico (NAFTA); and future trading blocs in the Pacific Basin between countries such as Japan, South Korea, Taiwan, Singapore, Thailand, Indonesia, and Malaysia.

In 1998 we saw the largest cross-national merger of two companies, when DiamlerChrysler was formed. In May 1998 when this merger took place it was the largest ever-industrial merger between two companies from different nations. Following on the heels of this merger British Petroleum and Amoco merged. This merger estimated at $113 billion is considered to be the biggest industrial transaction ever.

Along with the other factors listed above that promoted globalization, another significant factor is the advances that have been made in information technology. The merger of computer and communications technology has fueled globalization. Hammer and Mangurian (1987) talk about new systems called communications-intensive information systems (CIIS), that are being developed by organizations to impact the organization in terms of time compression, overcoming geographic restrictions, and restructuring of relationships within the organization. This has resulted in the possibility of a single world-wide information network that can be used to communicate data, voice, text, or images anywhere in the world (Deans & Ricks, 1993). The speed with which this network can be used for transmitting data in different forms enables globalization as information is moved from where it originates to where it is needed. No longer is physical presence a prerequisite for globalization. Amazon that began as a virtual bookstore in the United States is a prime example of a company that has become a major global organization without establishing physical infrastructure in different parts of the world. Global markets that are developing blur the national boundaries, as we know them. As a result no single country can afford to be isolated from the community of nations, because the world is characterized by global interdependence among all countries on the earth. Participation in global markets provides opportunities for developing and under-developed nations. Nations that do not participate in this economy will be isolated in the future.

IMPACT OF GLOBALIZATION ON EXECUTIVE DECISION-MAKING

As a result of globalization it becomes pertinent that executives working in global corporations assess organizational opportunities and threats in the global arena. Managing and controlling a diversified group of businesses that are spread around the world poses a major challenge for senior executives. An understanding of different national cultures, languages, competitive conditions, distribution channels, and political climate etc. become very important. This requires that relevant and accurate information must be made available to executives working in global corporations to assist them in decision-making. The reliability and accuracy of information can save a global organization significant time, money, and frustration leading to effective decision-making. Toffler (1991) says, " because it reduces the need for raw materials, labor, time, space, and capital, knowledge becomes the central resource of the advanced economy." Knowledge is accurate and reliable information that is provided to a decision-maker in a meaningful context.

Collecting and providing access to information for executive decision-making in a global environment is greatly enhanced with the use of information technology. In the past executive information systems (EIS), have been used by executives to help them in retrieving and analyzing relevant information required for decision-making. These systems that were developed in the early 1980s were designed to address the specific information needs of executives.

An EIS is defined as "a computer-based system that serves the information needs of top executives" (Turban, 1995, p. 403).

Watson, Rainer, and Koh (1991) define an EIS as a system that "provides executives with easy access to internal and external information that is relevant to their critical success factors" (p. 14).

This support has been limited in the past to executives working in organizations operating within national boundaries, primarily the United States. Most of the research in the EIS area has been conducted in the context of the domestic environment, for example, U.S. companies. Information pertaining to external environment of an organization, such as, competitors, customers, suppliers, government etc. is included in terms of a single country. The global environment of a company has not been included and/or investigated by researchers in the context of an EIS.

The globalization of business makes it imperative that senior executives have access to international information. This would be possible only if systems are developed that provide executives with such information. The internationalization of business firms and the increasing interdependence of firms in the global economy calls for the development of global executive information systems (global EISs) that will enable organizations to capture and use global information. In this book a global executive information system is defined as:

- a computer-based information system
- that provides easy access to internal and external information (both domestic and international)
- for senior executives working at headquarters and in subsidiaries worldwide of a global organization
- to support their analysis and decision-making functions.

The system uses databases (internal and external) to provide access to timely information. The global EIS is very user-friendly and access is provided via icons, a mouse and/or a touch screen. The user is not expected to have much IT or keyboarding skills. The information that is presented to the executives is supported by customized presentation formats (color and graphics) and provides exception reporting and drill-down capabilities. The system is linked to electronic mail and other online information services. Such a system would allow executives in global organizations to access data on markets worldwide. This will enable them to exploit opportunities, which will help the organization to achieve competitive advantages in different markets. Before a global EIS can be developed and potential benefits are derived, several problems need to be addressed. In this book, an attempt is made to explore the following research question:

What are the key issues in the design, development, structure, use and management of global executive information systems?

THE METHODOLOGY

The global EIS research study was conducted in three phases to address the research question addressed in the previous section. The three phases conducted for the study are: phase I: literature review and analysis, phase II: pilot case studies, and phase III: a pilot and the final mail survey.

Phase I of the research study (chapter 1) was an extensive literature review of the following streams of research: globalization and the role of information technology in global organizations, executive information systems and global executive information systems. The objective of the literature review was to propose a research framework for the study of global EIS (chapter 2). As a starting point the key international IS issues study (Deans et. al., 1991) was used to draw up a list of important issues for the study of information systems in global organizations. This study was then combined with the results of the Watson et al. (1991) study to identify issues for global executive information systems. This list of issues was then supplemented by other research studies in the international IS and executive information systems research streams (Carlyle, 1988; Deans & Kane, 1992; Eom, 1994; Freedman, 1985; Huff, 1991; Ives & Jarvenpaa, 1991; Ives, Jarvenpaa, & Mason, 1993; Leidner & Elam, 1993–94, 1994; Matthews & Shoebridge, 1992; Meall, 1990; Millet & Mawhinney, 1992; Palvia et al., 1992; Passino & Severance, 1990; Roche, 1992; Watson, 1995 etc.). The exhaustive list of issues drawn up from the literature review was then categorized using Deans and Ricks (1991), and Ives, et al. (1980) frameworks for research in international IS and management information systems. Watson et al. (1993) recommend using the Ives, et al. (1980) framework for the study of executive information systems. The resulting framework was used to develop a draft questionnaire for addressing the research question, i.e., identifying key issues for the design, development, structure, use, and management of global executive information systems.

Phase II of the research study used the case study approach to refine and extend the issues that were identified during the literature review. The objective of this phase was to use the case studies as a pilot to formulate specific research propositions and questions for the study. The first question that arises is why use case studies? There are two main reasons for using case studies for this research. Firstly, case studies would likely be the most appropriate way for initial investigation of issues in great depth for research in a relatively new area. This investigation will eventually form the foundation for further research in the area of global EIS. Secondly, as mentioned by Gummesson (1991), case study research provides the advantage of presenting a holistic view of a process. The in-depth investigation process allows us to study different aspects of a research topic and examine them in relation to each other. Further it enables us to view the total environment of the process under study. In the past case study research was not used very frequently. Gummesson (1991) points out the increasing use of case studies in management research. Bonoma (1985a, 1985b) talks about the trend towards greater use of case study research in the United States. Benbasat, Goldstein, and Mead (1987) provide suggestions for researchers who are interested in conducting case study research in information systems.

The next question that needs to be answered is what type of case study should be done? Yin (1984) distinguishes between three types of case study research: exploratory, descriptive, and explanatory. In this research study the case studies were primarily exploratory in nature. As mentioned earlier these case studies were used for formulating specific propositions and testable hypotheses for the research study. The data that was collected was analyzed using content analysis. Content analysis has been defined by Berelson (1952) as a process by which meaning of communication can be objectively and systematically portrayed. Coding of open-ended questions is pointed out as an example. Krippendorff (1980) describes content analysis as an exact procedure for making replicable and valid inferences from collected written or oral communication within the context from which it was obtained. In this study inferences were made based on the responses of the information systems executives. Underlying themes (Berelson, 1952) were the major unit of analysis. The results of this phase, alongwith the analysis of the literature, were used to draw research propositions and questions for the final study.

The case studies were conducted in five different companies based in Memphis, New York, and Los Angeles. Of the five companies used for the case study, four are U.S. based global organizations and one is a

Japanese company. The companies used in the study represent a variety of industries, such as, banking, entertainment, automobile, transportation and paper. Companies from both the service and manufacturing industry were included for the pilot case study. The companies for the pilot studies were not selected randomly. The selection of companies was based on the ability to gain access to senior IS executives of the company.

Every company used in the pilot study has operations in at least two countries, in other words, home country and outside the home country. Senior information systems executives (CIO, VP-Information systems etc.) were interviewed to elicit information for the case studies. Care was taken to ensure that the executives interviewed were involved with international IS projects and executive information systems projects in their respective companies. An open-ended questionnaire was used for these case studies.

Phase III of the research study used a mail survey to get responses. The objective of this phase was to verify the initial findings developed during the earlier phases (phase I and II). A multi-part questionnaire was mailed to a large random sample (503 companies) of geographically dispersed global firms in the United States. The mail questionnaire provided a definition of global executive information systems in the beginning to ensure that respondents have a basic understanding of the term and so that there is consistency in responses.

The first part of the questionnaire sought information relating to the design, development, use, and management of global executive information systems. The second part of the questionnaire tests relationships relating to the design and use of a global EIS. The third part of the questionnaire gathers demographic data on the responding organizations. The questionnaire was pretested by initially mailing it to 20 companies. Changes, if any, were incorporated and the questionnaire was then mailed to the remaining companies. The survey population for the questionnaire was chosen from the *Information Week* list of the 500 biggest and best corporate users of information technology. This list was matched with databases like the *World Directory of Multinational Enterprises* and the *Fortune Industrial and Service 5oo's* to develop a list of global organizations. It was assumed that being the leaders of the usage of information technology, these companies would be potential candidates to have a global EIS or an EIS. Once the data was collected, statistical tests were used to analyze the data and report the results (chapters 3, 4 and 5).

The respondents for this phase of the study included global companies headquartered in different parts of the United States and the world. Of the total usable responses (N = 48, approximately 9%), 86% of the companies had their headquarters in the United States and the remaining 14% had their headquarters in other countries of the world. The number of manufacturing sector companies was 23 and the number of service sector companies was 25. In the manufacturing sector companies, respondents included chemicals/health care, industrial, commercial electronics/computers, and consumer goods. The service sector category included companies from the following industries: transport, financial institutions, software development/consulting, telecommunications services, media, retail, pest control, and entertainment.

Fifty percent of the responding companies (N=34) have assets over $10 billion and the remaining companies had assets of less than $10 billion. Forty percent of the responding (N = 39) companies had revenues over $10 billion and the remaining 60% had revenues of less than $10 billion a year. The IS budget for the companies (N = 26) used in the study was between $100 million and $5 billion. Twenty-seven percent of the companies had an IS budget of over $1 billion, whereas the remaining 73% of the companies had an IS budget of less than $1 billion. All the 26 companies for which IS budgets are reported were included in the Information Week list of the biggest and best users of information technology.

The majority of the respondents (N = 45) for the study were Vice Presidents and/or Directors of the IS function in their respective organizations, followed by IS managers, CIO, Project leaders and consultants etc. The average total work experience of the respondents is 23 years, and the average IS experience of the respondents is 18 years (N = 43). Of the total companies that responded (N = 35), the average foreign involvement is 38% approximately. Foreign involvement is measured by dividing revenues from international operations by total revenue.

Fifty-seven percent of the companies (N = 47) responded in the positive when asked if they had an EIS being used in their companies. Twenty-eight percent of the companies (N = 47) responded that they use a global EIS for their senior executives. Only six of these companies answered about the scope of the system that was being used in these companies. In all six cases the global EIS was being used enterprise wide or all executives in the global organization were using the system.

Global Executive
Information Systems

CHAPTER 1

Role of Information Technology in Executive Decision-Making: Executive Information Systems

In 1982 Rockart and Treacy pointed out a trend of increased computer usage by CEOs in corporations. These computer-based information systems that were designed to support executives in an organization were called executive information systems. These systems were designed with the objective of overcoming the limitations provided by other computer-based information systems, i.e., management information systems (1960s) and decision support systems (1970s). Management information systems primarily provided a set of summarized reports and decision support systems were used specifically for analyzing decision-making tasks. Both these systems were being used mainly by the middle management in organizations. The advent of executive information systems in the late 70s and early 80s promised to provide support for executives, with little computing skills required of users. Today executive information systems are one of the fastest growing applications in U.S. organizations. Turban (1995) highlights the growth of EISs in the 1980s. He points out that by 1986 one-third of the large U.S. corporations were using EISs and the figure had risen to 50% in 1989.

DEFINITION OF EIS

A number of researchers have provided definitions for executive information systems. Turban (1995) defines an EIS as

3

"a computer-based system that serves the information needs of top executives. It provides rapid access to timely information and direct access to management reports. EIS is very user-friendly, supported by graphics, and provides exceptions reporting and "drill-down" capabilities. It is also easily connected with online information services and electronic mail" (p. 403).

Meall (1990) defines an EIS as "a resource tool; a system that delivers rapid access to the selected key information executives need for their decision making. Users should need no IT or keyboarding skills. Access is more likely to be via icons and a mouse or a touch screen, than a keyboard. Data is presented with the help of color and graphics, in a form which is highly structured and easy to understand" (p. 125).

Matthews and Shoebridge (1992) define an EIS as "a computer-based information delivery and communication system designed to support the needs of top executives" (p. 95).

Millet and Mawhinney (1992) define an EIS as "a system that integrates information from internal and external data sources enabling executives to monitor and request information of key importance to them via customized presentation formats" (p. 85).

CHARACTERISTICS/FEATURES OF EIS

The definitions in the previous section highlight some of the key characteristics of executive information systems. The characteristics/capabilities of executive information systems are:

- executive information systems are tailored to management style of individual executive users (Leidner & Elam, 1994; Turban, 1995; Watson et al., 1991)
- filters, compresses, and tracks critical data (Turban, 1995; Watson et al., 1991)

- provides drill-down capabilities to executives (Leidner & Elam, 1994; Matthews & Shoebridge, 1992; Meall, 1990; Moynihan, 1993; Turban, 1995; Watson et al., 1991)
- designed with managements critical success factors in mind (Houdeshel & Watson, 1987; Moynihan, 1993; Turban, 1995)
- status access, trend analysis, and exception reporting (Leidner & Elam, 1994; Matthews & Shoebridge, 1992; Turban, 1995; Watson et al., 1991)
- personalized analysis (Matthews & Shoebridge, 1992; Turban, 1995)
- navigation of information (Moynihan, 1993; Turban, 1995)
- provides access to and integrates internal and external data,i.e., aggregate (global) information (Houdeshel & Watson, 1987; Leidner & Elam, 1994; Meall, 1990; Moynihan, 1993; Turban, 1995; Watson et al., 1991)
- user-friendly and requires minimal or no training to use (Meall, 1990; Moynihan, 1993; Turban, 1995; Watson et al., 1991)
- used directly by executives without intermediaries (Houdeshel & Watson, 1987; Watson et al., 1991)
- present graphical, tabular, and/or textual information (Houdeshel & Watson, 1987; Matthews & Shoebridge, 1992; Turban, 1995; Watson et al., 1991)
- allows secure and confidential access to information (Matthews & Shoebridge, 1992; Turban, 1995)
- supports open-ended problem explanation (Moynihan, 1993; Turban, 1995)
- provides quick retrieval of desired information (Meall, 1990; Turban, 1995).

A brief description of some of the characteristics that are unique for an executive information system is provided below.

Drill-down capabilities: This capability of an EIS allows the executives to look for details on any specific information, for example, declining corporate sales in a particular region. Hypertext-style connections are used for accessing information, required by executives, in systems that support graphical user interface. Each level of detail that is accessed by the user may involve submenus if the system (or parts of it) is menu-driven.

Designed with management's critical success factors in mind: Every organization has certain critical factors that are important for achieving the organizational goals. These factors can be at the organizational level, departmental or division level, and individual level.

Status access, trend analysis, and exception reporting: This feature allows executives to access the current (latest) data on any key variable. The timing and relevance of information is very important. Trend analysis allows the executives to examine data across desired time intervals. Exception reporting allows the executives to highlight variances from established norms in a company. A brief description explaining the variance may also be provided.

Personalized analysis: This capability of an EIS allows executives to use built-in functions to analyze problematic situations. These functions allow the executives to specify the data that is required for processing the analysis and the format in which results are displayed.

Navigation of information: This feature allows the executives to access large amounts of data in a quick and efficient manner. Examples would include forward and backward path access, skipping screens while accessing a selected part of the system etc. Frolick and Ramarapu (1993) recommend the use of hypermedia to enhance this capability.

Presents graphical, tabular, and/or textual information: The information that is displayed on the terminal for executive users can be in several forms, such as, graphical, tabular, and/or textual information.

BENEFTS OF EIS

The use of executive information systems by executives provides several benefits for them. Some of the benefits of using an EIS mentioned in the literature (Armstrong, 1990; Houdeshel & Watson, 1987; Leidner & Elam, 1993–94, 1994; Turban, 1995; Watson et al., 1991) include:

- increases the quality of decision-making (i.e., fast decisions and actions)
- provides a competitive advantage
- meets the needs of executives
- more comprehensive analysis
- greater confidence

- improved service (speeding up of the flow of information)
- changing of the business focus
- saves time for user
- facilitates the attainment of organizational objectives
- provides better control in organizations
- improves communications (increase in capacity and quality)
- finds causes of problems

It is important to point out that these benefits can only be realized if executives support the EIS project and actively participate in the development of an EIS. Further, it is critical to understand that an EIS cannot possibly replace the intelligence of executives. These systems can only assist executives in providing information, which will enable them to be more effective in their decision-making functions. The final decisions are still made by the executives.

GLOBALIZATION AND EXECUTIVE DECISION-MAKING: THE ROLE OF INFORMATION TECHNOLOGY

> The business environment of present times is becoming increasingly complex and volatile, with sources for opportunities and threats becoming more diverse. (Ghoshal & Kim, 1986, p. 49)
>
> Competitive pressures are forcing all major firms to become global in scope and compete in multiple countries. (Carlyle, 1990, p. 25)

In recent years companies have started developing strategies to compete in the global market. The economic forces that are responsible for driving this strategic transformation in organizations are: economies of scale, economies of scope, potential for market growth, development of standardized global products, national differences in the availability and cost of productive resources, leveraging of scarce resources (management, equipment, and R&D etc.) and the need to satisfy the requirements of a worldwide customer (Bartlett & Ghoshal, 1992; Ives & Jarvenpaa, 1991). As a result of this strategic transformation researchers in management (Egelhoff, 1993; Ghoshal, 1987; Hout, Porter, & Rudden, 1982; Levitt, 1983; Perlmutter, 1969; Rowe, Mason, & Dickel, 1986; Yip, 1989) have presented different models of global business strategy. The trend of globalization, which is a dominating force in the 1990s, presents a set of challenges for organizations. Organizations have to compete with "foreign competitors who have different cultural, administrative, and physical resource bases and competencies" (Ghoshal & Kim, 1986, p. 49). In such a scenario the need for control, coordination and integration of activities in a global organization is enhanced (Bartlett & Ghoshal, 1987). Organizations operating in global markets can be at a strategic disadvantage if they do not control and coordinate their worldwide operations (Bartlett & Ghoshal, 1989). The control and coordination of activities in global organizations increases the need for information and the communication of this information between the headquarters of a company and its subsidiaries worldwide (Carlyle, 1988). Information technology can be of great use in such a scenario.

> Carefully crafted investments in global information technology (GIT) can offer firms an opportunity to increase control and enhance coordination while opening access to new global markets and businesses....Investments in information technology (IT) can provide direct competitive advantage in world markets. (Ives & Jarvenpaa, 1991, p.33)

The ever-increasing and irreversible phenomenon of globalization of businesses creates a tremendous need for information by these organizations. The potential use of information technology as a facilitator of globalization in undeniable. Several scholars (Deans & Kane, 1992; Deans, Karawan, Goslar, Ricks, & Toyne, 1991; Ives & Jarvenpaa, 1991; Palvia, Palvia, & Roche, 1996; Palvia, Palvia, & Zigli, 1992; Roche, 1992) in recent years have published on the issues that address the global deployment and development of information technology. Information technology in global organizations can be used to: *enhance competitive advantage* (Bartlett & Ghoshal, 1989; Farrell & Song, 1988; Galbraith, 1977; Ives & Jarvenpaa, 1991; Ives & Learmonth, 1984; Johnson & Vitale, 1988; Neo, 1991); *compress time and distance* (Hammer & Mangurian, 1987; Huff, 1991; Ives & Jarvenpaa, 1991); *control and coordinate activities in a global organization* (Huff, 1991; Ives & Jarvenpaa, 1991) and *knowledge sharing*.

Enhance competitive advantage: Several researchers in the past have talked about the role of information technology in providing competitive advantage to organizations. Parsons (1983) presented the impact of information technology on three levels, i.e., firm, industry, and strategy. Porter and Miller (1985) suggest that information technology can be used to coordinate the firm's value chain activities. Wiseman (1985) describes using information technology as a tool for gaining competitive advantage when it is used to support the competitive strategy of the firm. The use of information technology by global organizations enables them to gain a competitive advantage over local firms. Systems developed at headquarters may be deployed in different offices worldwide providing the company an advantage over local firms.

AMADEUS, a joint venture between SAS, British Airways, Lufthansa, Air France has developed a reservation system to corner the market share in Europe (Wiseman & MacMillan, 1984). This system was developed to achieve competitive advantage in the European market, just as American Airlines had achieved using SABRE.

Compress time and distance: Information technology used in global organizations greatly reduces time and distance by moving information from where it is generated to where it is needed for decision-making. The availability of information as and when required enables organizations to achieve advantages over their competitors.

SWIFT (Society for Worldwide Interbank Financial Telecommunications) is used by more than 1500 banks in approximately 70 countries for credit transfers (Ohmae, 1990). The system moves money freely and rapidly across national boundaries towards the investments with the greatest return.

Control and Coordinate Activities in a Global Organization: In a global marketplace the providers of goods and services and their consumers may be located in different places. Passino and Severance (1990) say that this can result in *"uncertainties and waste."* It becomes important to control and coordinate the activities that result in the transfer of these goods and services to their consumers. Information technology when used in such organizations can assist in reducing the inefficiencies caused by ineffective control and coordination. Simon, S.J. (as cited in Palvia, Palvia, & Roche, 1996) uses the concepts of control and coordination to illustrate strategies that a firm undertakes for achieving effective headquarter-subsidiary relationships.

> IBM is a company that manufactures, markets, and services their products around the world. The need for controlling and coordinating worldwide activities is very high. IBM has developed a system of linked databases and headquarters controlled lateral information flows. The system enables IBM to use their information infrastructure to achieve effective control and coordination worldwide. (Simon, S.J. as cited in Palvia, Palvia, and Roche, 1996).

> Buss (1982) provides an example of a senior regional executive in charge of operations in three different continents. The executive points out that "until three years ago my six European affiliates were very much self-contained operations. Today, however, I see these companies as an integrated set of manufacturing resources that supply different markets with products made wherever my cost advantage is the greatest." The information systems function, however, lacked this central coordination of data. Information was not available on time for effective decision-making.

> A more recent case is the classic example of the customization of products for customers in the apparel industry, e.g., Levi Strauss and Co. (Wiater, 1995). In some stores owned by the company customers can get measured for a custom pair of jeans. Once the order is taken the delivery of the product takes 2 to 3 weeks. The problems associated with high cost of inventory are reduced and information technology creates a world reach for an organization.

Knowledge Sharing (Sharing of scarce corporate expertise): Global companies would benefit a lot if they can use the expertise of their staff in different parts of the world. Every time customers' request for projects requiring the expertise of experienced staff members, it may not be possible physically to have experienced people available in different locations. Information technology can be used in such scenarios to provide customers the combined knowledge and expertise of the organization. This will not be possible for local firms, which will be limited to the expertise of the people who are located near the project.

> Price Waterhouse, one of the world's premier accounting and consulting firms, uses a proprietary, networked, global information system that collects, analyzes, and stores data from its worldwide staff. Consultants working on different projects worldwide document everything relating to a project on the system. The consulting staff at the company can also access outside information if required. Using this system Price Waterhouse consultants can offer their clients expert advice anywhere in the world in less than 24 hours. Knowledge dissemination within the organization is facilitated with the company gaining significant competitive advantages. (Laudon & Laudon, 1995)

GLOBAL EXECUTIVE INFORMATION SYSTEMS

Global executive information systems are a relatively new area of research and not much work has been done in this area. Palvia, Kumar, Kumar, and Hendon (1996) raise the issue that executive information systems being used by executives in global organizations need to be global in scope. They call a system developed specifically for this purpose a global EIS. In their paper, they conduct an exploratory study to identify in macro categories, the types of information required by executives in a global EIS, the current level of use of such information, and the sources of such information.

Watson (1995) points out that EIS development in other nations should be interesting to study. Comparisons of EISs developed in the U.S. and other countries would provide useful insights that can be used to develop global executive information systems by global companies. Some of the differences mentioned in the article include: objectives of developing EISs in the U.K. compared to the United States, the role of the IS department in the development of EISs in U.K., automatic currency conversion features, differences in international laws etc.

Eom (1994) talks about the emergence of "transnational management support systems" (TMSS) for organizations operating in the changing global environment. He defines the TMSS as:

An integrated system of decision support systems (DSS), expert systems (ES), and executive information systems (EIS). The TMSS supports the operational, tactical, and strategic decision-making process of multinational corporations in an attempt to integrate organizational decision-making across functional fields, planning horizons (long-, medium-, and short-range) and national boundaries. Such a system can best be designed as a network of management support systems (DSS, ES, EIS) that links a set of management support systems (MSS) in the headquarters with a set in each foreign and domestic subsidiary. (p. 23)

Eom (1994) highlights the significance of the EIS component in the TMSS, by saying that the EIS component is the major element for effectively collecting, analyzing and interpreting environmental scanning data for extracting meaningful information.

Min and Eom (1994) talk about developing an integrated decision support system (IDSS) for handling the complexities and the uncertainties of global logistics operations. They define such a system as:

A world-wide network of multi-user decision support systems that integrates the MNF's (multinational firm) various logistics operations and standardizes databases across national, cultural and market boundaries. The set of DSSs are linked electronically in the MNF's headquarters to a set of local DSSs located at foreign business partners, branch offices, suppliers and third-party logisticians. (p. 31)

A conceptual model of the system is presented in the paper. The components of the system include databases, model bases, dialog bases and knowledge bases. The authors point out that such a system "can be conceived as a viable strategic weapon for improving customer service, competitiveness, and economies of scale in transnational logistics operations" (Min & Eom, 1994, p. 31).

Jordan (1993) describes a prototype EIS developed for a regional CIO (Asia-Pacific) in a global organization. He makes the point that constructing a prototype for a CIO can be the first step in developing an enterprise-wide EIS for a global organization. A case study is presented in the paper, where the information requirements of the CIO are identified and a system is developed for the regional CIO. The author was involved in the requirements definition phase of the project as a participant observer. The prototype that was developed for the CIO was effective in meeting the information needs of the CIO and was described as being "valuable" to him. Sauter (1992) emphasizes that designers of transnational decision support systems should be sensitive to the differences among cultures when designing the model management component of a decision support system.

Violano (1988) describes Citicorp's Global Report System as one that provides executives with real time information on international banking. The system filters, integrates and organizes financial information (for example, international currency trading, foreign exchange, geographic countries and regions) for senior executives. Not only does the system provide information for executives, it also allows the user to search desired topics. This puts the "world, or at least a world of money market rates and foreign exchange data, at your fingertips" (p. 47) according to Violano.

Iyer and Schkade (1987) discuss different characteristics of multinational management support systems. They point out that managers of multinational corporations are often "inundated with unsolicited information from several sources" (p.63). It becomes important not only to retain such information, but also to organize it for future use. They propose the use of an ESS, which will not only allow executives to scan the information, but also perform ad-hoc analysis for evaluating decision tasks.

The studies mentioned in the preceding paragraphs do not provide a solid basis for research in global executive information systems. It is important to develop a framework that identifies the variables specific to the study of global executive information systems. In this research an attempt is made to develop such a framework. This framework identifies the variables and the key issues that need to be studied for global executive information systems. This framework should help researchers to conduct systematic research leading to the development of a cumulative body of knowledge in the area of global executive information systems. Further, unlike the case of executive information systems research, successful global EIS research can lead to successful global EIS practice.

CHAPTER 2

A Research Framework for Studying Global EIS

The foundation of any study is the research framework / model which provides direction for its conduct. Research frameworks that provide a basis for research in management information systems (Ein-Dor & Segev, 1978; Gorry & Morton, 1989; Ives, Hamilton, & Davis, 1980; Mason & Mitroff, 1973; Nolan & Wetherbe, 1980; Sprague, 1980; Watson et al., 1991 etc.) define the domain for conducting research in the field. All of these frameworks were developed with a view of understanding issues that are of importance to firms operating in one country, such as, the U.S. When a firm expands its operations to other parts of the world and becomes a global corporation, the IS function is influenced by a set of variables that are different from those encountered domestically. The above frameworks, however, fail to incorporate variables, which are unique to the global environment.

In this research study, the comprehensive computer-based information systems research framework proposed by Ives, Hamilton, and Davis (1980) was modified and extended to incorporate issues pertaining to international information systems and executive information systems. Watson et al. (1993) recommend using the Ives et al. (1980) framework for the study of the executive information systems. The objective is to identify the key issues in the design, development, structure, use and management of global executive information systems. The proposed framework is shown in Figure 1. This framework provides a meaningful foundation of the issues that are of importance for the study of global executive information systems.

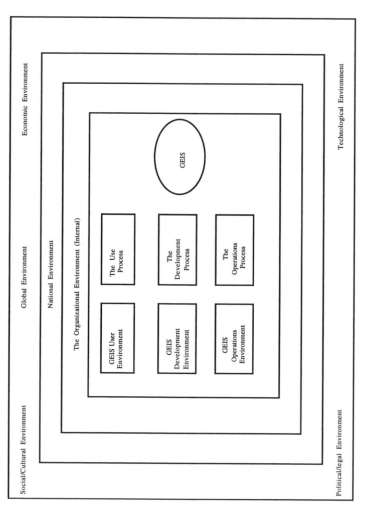

Figure 1: Global Executive Information Systems Research Framework

The thought process that was used to develop this framework is as follows. The global environment of the organization represents those variables that are unique in different countries, for example host countries where an organization operates. The impact of these variables on a global EIS is examined in this environment. The national environment depicts the home country, in this study primarily the U.S., of an organization. It interacts both with the global environment and the organizational environment. The organizational environment examines the impact that the usage of a global EIS has on an organization or the impact of the organization on the global EIS. The other variables used in the framework are for identifying users, developers, resources required and the attributes of the global EIS system.

The next section provides a description of the various components of the framework. The description for each component includes a set of research questions and representative research propositions for each category. These propositions are based on prior literature and the results of case studies conducted for this study. The propositions explain the various components of the model and the interactions within these components. Appropriate citations are provided for propositions that have been mentioned in the literature. The propositions that are based on the case studies results do not have any citations.

ENVIRONMENTAL VARIABLES

The survival and the growth of every organization are determined to a large extent by the resources available to an organization and the constraints imposed on the usage of these resources by an organization. These resources and constraints are a function of the environment in which an organization operates. Daft (1992) defines the organizational environment as "the different elements that exist outside the boundary of an organization and have the potential to affect all or part of the organization" (p. 71). Ball and McCulloch (1985) define the environment as the sum of all forces influencing the life and development of the firm, and they categorize these forces as external or internal. An organization needs to continually adapt to its environment in order to survive and grow. This adaptation process becomes further complicated when an organization operates in the global environment. This is due to the fact that factors in the global environment of an organization may not be controllable directly by an organization, even though they influence the working of the organization. This implies that factors that are a part of the internal environment of an organization must be managed effectively in order to adequately control factors in the external environment. The external environmental variables that are incorporated in the framework include the global environment and the national environment. The internal environmental variables incorporated in the framework include organizational environment, global EIS user environment, global EIS development environment, and global EIS operations environment.

THE GLOBAL ENVIRONMENT

Forces that are unique in different countries where an organization operates characterize the global environment of an organization. These forces can be categorized on the basis of the following differences: governments, regulations, cultures, education, economies, the level of sophistication of the IT infrastructure available, currencies, languages, and measurement units etc. Each of these differences that exists place a constraint on the resources that are available to an organization to operate in different parts of the world. Deans and Ricks (1991) categorize these forces into four dimensions, namely, social/cultural, economic, political/legal, and technological (Figure 1). They emphasize that it is important to recognize demands imposed by these environmental forces on executive decision making. They further point out executives must learn to recognize those factors that are fixed, those that are changeable and those that are most critical in each of these dimensions. The factors that can be influenced are the ones that need to be focused on and the impact of the other factors should be understood.

The dimensions of the global environment, stated above, raise certain basic issues for the design, development, use and management of a global EIS. The following paragraphs list research questions and propositions that reflect the importance of the global environment.

Social/Cultural environment: It is important for senior executives working in a global organization to understand the role of information technology. This understanding should not be limited to executives working at the headquarters only. Senior executives working worldwide in subsidiaries of a global organization should be aware of the potential of using information technology. This is especially true in case of executives working in subsidiaries located in developing countries. The success of a global executive information system could depend to a large extent on the awareness (education) of these executives.

Proposition: The greater the level of executive awareness (education) of the potential use of information technology in different countries (especially developing) the greater will be the diffusion/usage of global EIS in a global organization. (Buss, 1982; Deans et al., 1991)

The power distance norm (Hofstede, 1980) shows the differences in cultures with respect to the distribution of power of members in the organizations and societies in different parts of the world. Nations with a high power distance (such as India, Philippines, Hong Kong etc.) do not readily accept technologies (for example global EIS) which might bring about a change in the distribution of power of its members. Information systems, which might be perceived to reduce the power distance structure in organizations and society, will not be readily accepted in such societies.

Proposition: Information technology (such as global EIS) that might be perceived to introduce significant changes in the distribution of power and status of executives in an organization, located in countries that emphasize power distance, is less likely to be effectively used. (Kedia & Bhagat, 1988)

Political/legal environment: This environment is a function of the different governments that a global organization has to negotiate with to operate in different parts of the world. How do foreign governments view international organizations operating in their countries and the legal restrictions and demands that they impose on their operations are the main issues for global organizations. Differences in legal restrictions that may apply to global organizations include among others, the restrictions imposed on transborder data flows, acquisition of hardware and software from outside the country, and the usage of telecommunications equipment.

Transborder data flow restrictions imposed by governments is a major constraint faced by global organizations. Transmitting data from where it originates to the place where it is required for decision-making is very important for controlling and coordinating the operations of a global organization. Carlyle (1988) points out that "on the congested data highways of multinational corporations, the problems of getting the right data in the right amount to the right people at the right time are multiplying daily as global markets emerge" (p.54). The establishment of communications networks worldwide ensures that data transmission problems are reduced to the greatest extent possible. However, regulations imposed by nations that restrict the movement of data across borders are a major hurdle in the effective use of such networks.

> Proposition: The greater the extent of regulations (restrictions) imposed on transborder data flows, acquisition of hardware and software, and the usage of certain telecommunications equipment by nations, the less effective will be the diffusion/usage of information technologies (such as global EIS) in a global organization operating in these nations. (Buss, 1982; Deans et al., 1991)

Economic environment: The economic characteristics that are of concern for the development and use of information technology in a global organization are the stability of the national economic infrastructure and the currency restrictions that are imposed on the purchase of technological equipment in a country. Both the factors are very important for the successful usage of systems (such as global EIS) in global organizations.

> Proposition: The more stable the national economic infrastructure of a country is, where a global organization operates, the more effective will be the usage of information technologies (such as global EIS) by executives in global organizations. (Deans et al., 1991).

> Proposition: The greater the exchange (currency) restrictions imposed on the purchase of technological equipment in a country, the less likely will be the usage of information technology (such as global EIS) by executives working in that country. (Deans et al., 1991).

Technological environment: The information technology infrastructure available in a country and the level of sophistication of the IT infrastructure are key issues for the successful usage of IT in a global organization. The IT infrastructure available in different parts of the world will determine the ability of the global organization to provide continuing support for technologies that are being used. The lack of an IT infrastructure will create major obstacles for the use of technology.

Proposition: The better the information technology infrastructure availability and sophistication in a country is, the greater the chances of success for information technology (such as global EIS) usage by executives in global organizations operating in such countries. (Buss, 1982; Deans et al., 1991)

In addition to some of the issues addressed above there are several characteristics that need to be looked at for developing a global EIS. These characteristics vary with nations where a global company operates and should be incorporated in the global EIS.

Q.1. What are the features that are desirable in a global executive information system (reflecting differences in languages, currencies, measurement unit's etc.)?

NATIONAL ENVIRONMENT

The national environment identifies the home country, for example the U.S., of an organization. This environment depicts the interactions between the organization and its customers, suppliers, competitors, government, economic conditions, etc. It is important to recognize the demands imposed by environmental forces in the national environment, on executive decision making.

The various factors in the national environment, which impose demands on the organization, create a need for information and resources from the environment. The information and resources required from the environment change with the level of uncertainty in the environment. An organization must adapt itself to the change in the environmental uncertainty for its continued survival and growth. It is this need for information and resources that led to the development of executive information systems (EIS), during the eighties, in the United States. Considerable amount of research has already been done in the area of EIS (Chapter 1) within United States. The issues that are of importance for the design, development and use of a global EIS within the national environment of a global organization are as follows:

Q.2. What are the different external sources of information that can be used for a global executive information system?

Proposition: The greater the intensity of the global competition that an organization faces, in its national environment (home country), the greater will be the demand for external sources of information for a global EIS.

Proposition: The greater the governmental constraints imposed on the acquisition of information by organizations (in home country), the less likely it is that the quality of information in a global EIS would be effective/good.

Proposition: The greater the level of uncertainty in the national environment of an organization, the greater will be the demand for external information for a global EIS.

ORGANIZATIONAL ENVIRONMENT (INTERNAL)

Daft (1992) defines an organization as "social entities that are goal-directed, deliberately structured activity systems with an identifiable boundary." The boundary identifies the elements, which are within the organization (internal), and those elements that are a part of its external environment. The internal elements identified by the organizational environment are the organizational mission, goals, tasks, objectives, management philosophy, organizational structure etc. For example, the span of control in an organization may be reflected in the information flows in an organization. The extent of standardization in an organization may be reflected in standards being established for information systems development, across the organization.

The absorption of information technology (such as global EIS) in a global organization changes the "anatomy of the corporation and the mindset of its people" (Passino & Severance, 1990, p. 76). It becomes important to identify and understand the potential impact that the usage of a global EIS has on the organization, for example organizational strategy, organizational structure, organizational learning, organizational design etc. Not only do we need to identify and understand the impact of the usage of a global EIS, it is important to prepare the people who will be impacted by the change. If the people (executives) are not prepared and willing to accept this change, the introduction of a global EIS will not be successful. The issues that are of importance and need to be explored are:

Q.3. How does the usage of a global executive information system impact the organization?

The position of information systems within the global organization affects the effectiveness of the usage of information technology in such organizations. Buss (1982) talks about the lack of integration of business objectives and information systems plans at different levels (global, regional, and country) in an organization. This lack of integration can confuse IS managers in global organizations. Reck (1989) says that it is important for information systems strategies in global organizations to be in line with the basic organizational strategy. Ives and Jarvenpaa (1991) point out that "misalignment of information technology with global business strategy can severely hamper a firm's efforts to seek global pre-eminence" (p. 34).

Proposition: The effectiveness of the global EIS in a global organization will be greater if the global EIS supports the overall organizational strategy (Ives & Jarvenpaa, 1991).

Investments made in information technology by global organizations will tend to be sizable, especially in the early years. The potential benefits that are derived by using information technology will be enhanced by the extent of usage of the technology by executives in a global organization.

Proposition: The value of global EIS investments for a global organization will increase with the diffusion of the system.

GLOBAL EIS USER ENVIRONMENT

The user environment is used to identify the scope of the global EIS that is developed for the users, the primary users of the global EIS, and the involvement of senior executives in the initiation and sponsorship of the global EIS project. It becomes important to determine the scope of the global EIS project at the beginning of the development process. Wetherbe (1991) points out those revisions that are required to be made to an EIS are very expensive. This necessitates that an organization should decide up-front whether a global EIS should be developed for the global organization or should a global EIS be developed for regional areas in a global organization, for example Asia-Pacific, Europe etc. Other possibilities that can be explored by organizations are to develop a global EIS for a specific product division and/or a department/functional unit for the entire organization. Watson et. al. (1991) point out the existence of EIS that are developed for functional areas rather than for an organization.

Q.4. What should be the scope of the global executive information system?

The scope of the system that is developed will determine to a large extent on the primary users of the system, executive decision-makers (senior and/or middle management) at headquarters and subsidiaries. If middle management at headquarters and subsidiaries are to be included as primary users of the system, then job functions, work styles, and support needs of these users will have to be taken into account (DeLong & Rockart, 1992) for developing the system.

Q.5. Who are the primary users of the global executive information system?

A global EIS is a system developed primarily for senior executives in a global organization. The question that arises is who should initiate the project: senior executives or the IS function in an organization? Systems that are initiated and motivated by executives will have better chances of success, as they are the users.

Proposition: Initiation of the global EIS project by business executives (functional heads or CEO, rather than IS personnel) will increase the chances of success of the system (global EIS).

Proposition: The higher the organizational level of the initiator of the global EIS project, the better the chances of its being successful (Watson et al., 1991).

Every system that is developed in an organization needs a sponsor to ensure that the project is implemented successfully. The literature (Barrow, 1990; Rockart & DeLong, 1988) identifies an executive sponsor for the development of an EIS. This person is a senior executive in the organization and is primarily responsible for initiating the system. This person supervises the development of the system providing feedback for applications, and communicating a strong interest to those people who have a stake in the system, such as staff and managers who provide data for the system. The executive sponsor being a senior executive may not be able to dedicate sufficient time for supervising the implementation of the system. In such a case an operating sponsor (Rockart & DeLong, 1988) can be designated. This person is an executive who has an interest in the successful implementation of the system and is familiar with the work style of the executive sponsor. The position of the sponsors (executive and operating) in a global organization will determine to a large extent the success of the system and leads to the following propositions.

Proposition: The higher the organizational level of executive sponsorship, the greater is the degree of success of the global EIS (Watson et al., 1991).

Proposition: The higher the organizational level of operating sponsorship, the greater is the degree of success of the global EIS (Watson et al., 1991).

GLOBAL EIS DEVELOPMENT ENVIRONMENT

This environment identifies the assigning of responsibilities for planning the development of the global EIS, the methodologies and techniques for determining information requirements and the development of a global EIS, in-house versus customized development of the global EIS, and the characteristics of the development team and its members. It is important to identify at the beginning of any project the people who should be responsible for planning the development of the system. As a global EIS is intended for use by senior executives, working worldwide in a global organization, the process of planning the project and assigning responsibilities becomes even more complex and significant. The person(s) who are assigned this responsibility should ensure that the global EIS is developed keeping in mind the overall objectives of the global organization. Buss (1982) points out that an "international computer council" should be created to develop plans for international information systems and to ensure that they are compatible with corporate objectives.

> Q.6. Who is responsible for planning the development of the global executive information system?

A key issue in developing information systems for executives is making sure that their requirements are fulfilled by the system. Wetherbe (1991) points out that a lot of the systems (EIS) fail because the requirements of executives are not met adequately. He talks about the different approaches that can be used for getting executive information requirements correctly. Watson and Frolick (1992) discuss several strategies in their paper for determining information requirements. They point out that determining an executive's information requirements can be a difficult task. Identifying information requirements for an EIS has been ranked as the number one concern in several studies (Paller, 1990; Stecklow, 1989; Watson & Frolick, 1992). This makes it critical to identify the methodologies that can be used for determining and validating information requirements for a global EIS.

> Q.7. What methodology should be used to determine and validate information requirements for a global executive information system?

The methodology used to develop a global EIS is important because of the specific requirements/needs of executives. The choices can vary from using the traditional long-term approach (SDLC) to an iterative approach, i.e., prototyping. The time taken to develop the first version of the system is the major factor. The literature (Moad, 1988; Rainer & Watson, 1995; Runge, 1988) points out the importance of delivering the first EIS application quickly so that executives are interested in the project. This implies that using a development methodology which helps creating the first application quickly may be more desirable for developing a global EIS.

Q.8. What methodology should be used to develop a global executive information system?

A global EIS can be developed in-house, customization of off-the shelf software, a combination of the two or using off-the shelf software (Paller & Laska, 1990 as cited in Watson et al. 1991; Rockart & DeLong, 1988). The availability of several EIS products in the market (Comshare EIS, IBM Office Vision, Pilot Command Center, Digital DEC Decisions in Nord & Nord, 1995; and EXECUCOM-Executive Edge and IBM-Executive Decisions in Watson et al., 1991) may make it attractive to customize these products to incorporate the international dimensions for a global EIS.

Q.9. How should the global executive information system be developed (in-house vs customization of off the shelf software product)?

Whether it is an in-house effort or a customization of an EIS product, it is important to identify the people who should be involved with the development of a global EIS, the skills that they should have, and the number of people that should be there on the development team. It becomes even more important in the context of a global organization because team members can be from different parts of the world. A system that is developed by headquarters staff may not be acceptable in subsidiaries. Buss (1982) points out that it is crucial for organizations to overcome the *'not invented here'* syndrome and convince country managers that it makes business sense to use application programs developed elsewhere.

Q.10. Who should develop the global executive information system? Where should the system be developed?

Q.11. What are the skills required of members on the global EIS development team?

GLOBAL EIS OPERATIONS ENVIRONMENT

This environment identifies the resources required to operate the global EIS. The resources required include hardware, software, databases, documentation (procedures), information processing centers, and the secondary personnel for the global EIS. All efforts must be made by a global organization to ensure that adequate resources are available for successfully using a global EIS.

Rockart and DeLong (1988) point out that there are several hardware configurations that are possible for an EIS. Watson et. al. (1991) found out the following hardware configurations in their study: mainframe approach and the PC network approach. Turban (1995) points out four different hardware alternatives for using an EIS: mainframes with graphical terminals (dumb); mainframes with PCs for user interface; LAN-based PCs for departments; and an enterprise-wide network. In the case of a global EIS several countries are involved and selecting a hardware configuration can be a difficult task. Ideally speaking, as mentioned by Freedman (1985), subsidiaries in global organizations should be able to use the same hardware purchased from the same vendor, common application packages and a network that ties everything together. However, in reality it is very difficult to achieve this. The question that needs to be examined is whether these alternatives are feasible for a global EIS.

Q.12. What should be the hardware configuration for using a global executive information system?

In the global EIS development environment it was mentioned that a global EIS could be developed in-house or by customizing off-the-shelf software. A combination of both approaches is also possible. Care must be taken to ensure that the system includes features that pertain to the international environment. Executives in subsidiaries of a global organization would more readily use a system that is customized to include local features in the software, such as language, currency, measurement units etc. (Buss 1982). This leads to the following proposition.

Proposition: A customized global EIS (software) for executives in
different parts of the world will lead to greater acceptance of the
system.

Several different possibilities exist with respect to the databases
(internal) that are used for a global EIS. The database organization can
be centralized, decentralized, or distributed. Since executives
worldwide will access the data, we propose that:

Proposition: Standardized distributed databases are more appropriate
for a global EIS.

The global EIS developed for use by executives may include
people from different parts of the organization and countries. It is
necessary that adequate documentation is provided for such a system.
Lack of documentation can lead to numerous problems with the
maintenance of the system. This leads to the next proposition.

Proposition: The greater the extent of documentation of the global
EIS, the easier it will be to maintain the system.

As Carlyle (1988) points out, the evolutionary process of
organizations towards globalization is dependent on networks to some
extent. As an organization moves towards becoming global in scope it
becomes important to ensure that data can be transmitted between the
different centers of operation. This transmission of data between
different operational centers of an organization can be critical for
management decision-making. Not only does an organization need to
have a network in place for data transmission, alternate facilities should
be identified to ensure continuous transmission if the organization is to
compete with other global companies. It becomes important for global
organizations to identify suitable information processing locations
worldwide to enable the movement of data between those locations.
These worldwide information processing locations will integrate
networks for linking of dispersed operations to enable coordination and
control in global organizations. The issue that needs to be explored is:

Q.13. Where does a global company operate information processing
centers for effective transmission of data?

A global EIS that utilizes data from subsidiaries worldwide necessitates that adequate support is provided throughout the organization. This support is required with respect to secondary users of the system, such as the personnel used for data entry, etc. and the operational staff. These people ensure that the system is always functional and at the same time maintain the data that is required for a global EIS. It is important to provide support in the subsidiaries of a global organization to ensure that the system is reliable and operational all the time. If the system does not provide executives with the information that they need on time (Wetherbe, 1991), the system will not be useful.

> Proposition: Localized (in subsidiaries) support staff (both technical and data entry) is essential for a global EIS.

THE PROCESS VARIABLES

As described by Ives et al. (1980) the process variables comprise the interactions between the global EIS and the environments. The process variables represent the measures of these interactions. The categories of process variables as shown in Figure 1 are: the global EIS use process, the global EIS development process, and the global EIS operations process. In the following sections a description of each of these process variables is provided alongwith research propositions and questions.

The Global EIS Use Process

The use process describes the actual usage of the global EIS by executives, who are the primary users in an organization. The usage process is measured by the impact on executive work due to the usage of a global EIS. Several studies (Elam & Leidner, 1995; Nord & Nord, 1995; Rainer & Watson 1995; Watson et al., 1991) in recent years have examined the impact of using an EIS on the work of an executive. All these studies were conducted in the context of a system, the EIS that was developed and used in the domestic environment, for example the United States. It becomes important to identify the impact that the use of a global EIS will have on the work of an executive.

Q.14. How does the use of a global EIS impact the work of an executive?

As described in the previous paragraph the usage of a global EIS impacts the work (decision-making) of an executive. Davis and Olson (1985) point out that the information satisfaction resulting from the quality of information provided can be used to measure the output (decisions) of the system. The case studies conducted showed that the improvement in decision-making, due to information satisfaction of executives, impacts the satisfaction of executives and leads to the following proposition.

Proposition: The greater the quality of the decision-making is, resulting from the usage of the global EIS by executives, the greater will be the satisfaction of executives.

The Global EIS Development Process

The development process of a global EIS utilizes organizational resources to create the system. The organizational resources that are used in the process include the extent and level of participation by the users (primary and secondary), the cost that is incurred to develop the system and the time taken for developing a global EIS. As Wetherbe (1991) points out "most information systems do not meet executive needs" (p. 51). This is primarily due to the fact that users (executives) are not actively involved in the development process and leads us to the next propositions.

Proposition: Active participation by executives (primary users) in the development process of the global EIS will lead to a better quality system being developed.

Proposition: Active participation by secondary users (operations and maintenance personnel) in the development process of the global EIS will lead to a better quality system being developed.

A system that meets the needs of the executives should lead to greater satisfaction. It will also ensure that adequate funding is provided by executives for the development of the system and leads us to the following propositions.

> Proposition: Active participation by executives in the development process of the global EIS will lead to greater satisfaction with the system (in turn increasing the chances of success of the system).
>
> Proposition: Active participation by executives in the development process will ensure adequate funding for the project.

An important measure of the development process of a global EIS is the cost associated with developing the system. Watson et al. (1991) identified two categories of cost for developing an EIS, development and operational cost. In each case the costs are classified into hardware, software, training and personnel. It is important to find out the costs that are associated with developing a global EIS.

> Q.15. What are the costs associated with the development of a global EIS?

The difficulty of quantifying benefits (Houdshel & Watson, 1987; Moad, 1988; Rockart & DeLong, 1988; Rockart & Treacy, 1982) for an EIS are pointed out in the literature. Watson et al. (1991) mentions "intuitive feelings about improved decision-making" as one of the benefits of using an EIS. In other sections an attempt to explore the impact on the work of an executive and the organization have been made. These benefits though intangible will justify the cost incurred on developing a global EIS.

> Proposition: The benefits of using a global EIS will justify the cost spend on developing the global EIS (Watson et al., 1991).

Watson et al. (1991) highlight the significance of determining the time taken to develop an EIS. If the development process is too long users may loose interest and the project may be a failure.

> Q.16. What is the time taken to develop the global EIS?

The Global EIS Operations Process

The operations process refers to the physical operation of the global EIS and is primarily a function of the operations resource. The operations process is measured by the reliability of the system (global EIS), the response and adaptability of the system to incorporate changing information requirements, and the problems associated with global EIS spread and evolution. Issues that need to be identified and explored are:

Proposition: High error rates (inaccurate information etc.) in the usage of the global EIS will lead to dissatisfied users.

Proposition: The greater the flexibility of the global EIS to incorporate changing requirements, the greater will be the satisfaction of the users. (Rainer & Watson, 1995; Watson et al., 1993; Wetherbe, 1991)

Proposition: An increase in the number of executive users of a global EIS will lead to better chances of success for the global EIS. (Friend, 1990; Watson et al., 1991)

Proposition: An increase in the number of executive users of a global EIS will lead to an increase in the number of screens (more information) demanded by executives. (Watson et al., 1991)

Spread of an EIS is defined by Rockart and DeLong (1988) as an increase in the number of users accessing the EIS. They point out that an increase in users will occur when information reflecting the performance of subordinates is accessible by executives. Rockart and DeLong (1988) say the demand for additional capabilities of an EIS goes up as users become familiar with the system. They define this as the evolution of the system.

GLOBAL EXECUTIVE INFORMATION SYSTEM ARCHITECTURE

The GEIS in the framework (Figure 1) represents the output of the development process. This output represents the architecture of the global EIS (Figure 2) and is composed of the following components: data management, knowledge management, model management, presentation format, and the user-interface. In addition to these components it is important to mention here that the global EIS also interacts with other computer-based information systems in an organization to provide information to executives for effective decision-making. A description of the components of the global EIS with research questions follows.

DATA MANAGEMENT

The data management component of the global EIS architecture includes the internal and external databases, which are used to provide relevant information to the executives for effective decision-making. The external sources that an organization needs to access for meeting its requirements are discussed in the national environment.

The internal sources of data for a global organization would include data at headquarters and subsidiaries worldwide. This data would be extracted from the transaction processing systems in different functional areas of a business (Watson et al., 1991). The issue of concern for the developers of a global EIS is the scope of the data that is to be included in the global EIS from internal sources.

Q.17. What is the scope of the data that is to be included in a global EIS?

The data in the data management component of the global EIS are managed by a database management system. As this data pertains to headquarters and subsidiary operations, it is important to identify the problems that might be encountered with respect to managing this data. Issues that will be of concern for database administrators will be the integrity, security, and standards for the data that is a part of data management.

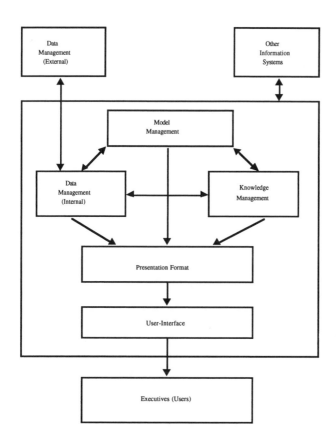

Figure 2: Global Executive Information System Architecture

Q.18. What are the potential problems in a global EIS with respect to data management?

Another concern for the database administrator would be the inclusion of soft data in this component. Watson et al. (1991) recommend that it is important for an organization to include soft data (news, rumors etc.) as a part of the internal databases for an EIS. It would be interesting to see if including soft data in a global EIS would improve the quality of the system.

Proposition: Inclusion of soft data in the global EIS will improve the quality of the global EIS (Mintzberg, 1975; Watson et al., 1991; Zmud 1986).

Knowledge management

A global organization operates in an unstable, dynamic, heterogeneous, dispersed, complex, and turbulent environment. These conditions make the decision-making environment very unstructured and traditional models used by executives may not suffice in such a case. Knowledge from experts in domains that are specific to the international environment, for example international laws and regulations, can be captured in this component of the global EIS. The knowledge management component can be extended to include explanation and learning capabilities to assist executives in getting a better understanding of the international environment. The knowledge that is stored in this component is managed by a knowledge base management system. Including rules, facts and heuristics will improve the quality of the system that is developed and leads to the next proposition.

Proposition: Inclusion of executive expertise in the global EIS will enhance the quality of the system. (Eom, 1994; Min & Eom, 1993; Turban, 1995)

Model management

This component of the global EIS provides a database of different models that can be used by executives for evaluating alternative courses of action. Executives need to evaluate several courses of action before they finally make a decision to go along with any one of the options. These models can be either task oriented or function oriented. Examples of such models are statistical, financial, analytical, forecasting, mathematical, inventory, quantitative, simulation, logistics, transportation models etc. All these different models can be linked to each other so that executives can use any one of these models based on their needs. This leads to the next proposition:

> Proposition: A model base incorporated in the global EIS will increase the effectiveness of the system. (Eom, 1994; Min & Eom, 1993; Turban, 1995)

Presentation format

This component represents the format in which information is displayed for the executive user. Information presentation in a desired format for executives in a global company should be customized for individual users (executives) worldwide. This customization should facilitate the multilingual and multicultural aspects of the work of executives worldwide.

> Proposition: Customization of the global EIS for individual users (e.g. executives in different parts of the world) in a global organization will lead to greater usage of the system.

The global EIS should be easy-to-use so that executives can use it easily. Graphics and color along with tabular presentation of information are important. Features that allow electronic mail to be integrated with the information presented in different formats should be incorporated. Executives should be able to schedule appointments using this component of the global EIS.

> Q.19. What are the features that are required to present information to executives using a global EIS?

User-interface

The interactive communication that takes place between the executives and the global EIS is very important from the users point of view. Executives may not be willing to use the keyboard for interacting with the system. GUI based interaction will be more easily accepted by executives. The interaction should be on-line for executives so that they do not have to wait for the information that they need. If the response time for getting the information is long, executives may not want to use the system frequently.

Proposition: Menus and icons will be preferred by executives over command languages in a global EIS. (Watson et al., 1991).

Proposition: A global EIS with slow response time will lead to dissatisfied executive users. (Houdshel & Watson, 1987; Rockart & DeLong, 1988; Watson et al., 1991)

CHAPTER 3

The Global EIS Environment

The global environment, which is the outermost layer in the framework, identifies the forces that are unique to different countries where an organization operates. These forces impact the development, usage and diffusion of a global EIS in a global organization. The results of the issues that are important and impact the development, usage and diffusion of a global EIS in the global environment of an organization are presented in Table 1.

Social/Cultural

> Proposition: The greater the level of executive awareness (education) of the potential use of information technology in different countries (especially developing) the greater will be the diffusion/usage of GEIS in a global organization. (Buss, 1982; Deans et al., 1991)

> Proposition: Information technology (i.e., GEIS) that might be perceived to introduce significant changes in the distribution of power and status of executives in an organization, located in countries that emphasize power distance, is less likely to be effectively used. (Kedia & Bhagat, 1988)

Respondents agree that executive education (81.3%) in different parts of the world will impact the usage/diffusion of a GEIS in a global company. As the literature (Buss, 1982; Deans et al., 1991; Palvia, Palvia, and Roche, 1996) suggests executive education is an important criteria for the successful usage/diffusion of a system in a global company. This issue will have a greater impact in subsidiaries of a

Table 1 Key issues for the usage/diffusion of a GEIS in a global company

Issues	Agree/ strongly agree %	Neither agree/ or disagree %	Disagree/ strongly disagree %
Social/Cultural:			
Executive education	81.3	10.3	8.4
Distribution of power	45.9	35.4	18.7
Technological:			
IT infrastructure availability	73.0	12.5	14.5
Political/Legal:	47.9	22.9	29.2
Regulation of TBDF, acquisition of hardware/software and usage of telecommunications equipment			
Economic:			
Stability of national economy	25.0	41.7	33.3
Exchange (currency) restrictions on purchase of technological equipment	29.2	18.8	52.0

global organization that are located in the developing world. As Palvia, et al. (1996), point out "an appreciation of the benefits and potential applications of MIS is absolutely necessary for successful IT deployment" (p. 16).

The usage and diffusion of a system, such as a global EIS that is perceived to bring a change in the distribution of power of members within an organization, is less likely to be effectively used, is considered to be a moderately important issue (45.9%). The literature (Kedia & Bhagat, 1988; Palvia, et al. 1996, p. 19) points out the significance of this cultural dimension with respect to diffusion of technology in developing countries. Only 18.7% of the respondents disagree with this statement. A possible explanation of the not so high importance of this issue may be the successful diffusion of technology in nations with a high power distance (such as India) in recent years.

Technological

> Proposition: The better the information technology infrastructure availability and sophistication in a country is, the greater the chances of success for information technology (global EIS) usage by executives in global organizations operating in such countries. (Buss, 1982; Deans et al., 1991)

More than two-thirds of the respondents (73.0%) agree that the level and sophistication of the IT infrastructure available will impact the usage and success of systems (global EIS) in different parts of the world. This is especially true in cases where subsidiaries are located in the developing and under-developed countries (Buss, 1982; Deans et al., 1991; Palvia, et al., 1996, p. 17 and 21) and is consistent with the literature. For these countries the issue of significance is to create the infrastructure required for successful usage of IT before systems can be implemented.

Political/Legal

> Proposition: The greater the extent of regulations (restrictions) imposed on transborder data flows, acquisition of hardware and software, and the usage of certain telecommunications equipment by nations, the less effective will be the diffusion/usage of information

technologies (global EIS) in a global organization operating in these nations. (Buss, 1982; Deans et al., 1991)

The regulations that are imposed on transborder data flows (TBDFs), acquisition of hardware and software, and the usage of telecommunications equipment will impact the usage of a global EIS in a global company, though only moderately (47.9%). With more and more nations removing restrictions on the acquisition of technology, the impact of political/legal restrictions will continue to be less important in the future. The only places where political influences may still be an important issue will be in subsidiaries located in underdeveloped countries (Palvia, et al., 1996, p. 21), and in unstable political environments.

Economic

> Proposition: The more stable the national economic infrastructure of a country is, where a global organization operates, the more effective will be the usage of information technologies (global EIS) by executives in global organizations. (Deans et al., 1991)

> Proposition: The greater the exchange (currency) restrictions imposed on the purchase of technological equipment in a country, the less likely will be the usage of information technology (global EIS) by executives working in that country. (Deans et al., 1991)

Very few of the respondents feel that the stability of the national economy of a country (25.0%) and the exchange (currency) restrictions imposed on the purchase of technological equipment (29.2%) has an impact on the usage/diffusion of a GEIS in a global company. In recent years, with the opening up of the eastern bloc of nations, the break-up of the former USSR, and the increased use of technology in developing countries, restrictions have been removed, facilitating the easy acquisition of technology. More and more nations are realizing that technology is very important for the growth and progress of a nation. This could be a possible explanation for the respondents' opinion with respect to economic factors.

Q. What are the features that are desirable in a global executive information system (reflecting differences in languages, currencies, measurement unit's etc.)?

Another important aspect of the global environment that may potentially impact the usage/diffusion of a global EIS, are the features that are desired by executives worldwide in a global organization. The literature review and case study results were used to identify three main features, desired in a global EIS, by executives working in a global organization. Table 2 provides the results of these features.

Table 2 Features of a GEIS desired by executives worldwide

Features desired	Imp./very imp. %	Somewhat imp. %	Not imp./ of little imp. %
Inclusion of different currencies	56.2	31.3	12.5
Multi-lingual capabilities	33.3	41.7	25.0
Inclusion of different measurement units (e.g. metric system)	33.3	35.4	31.3

Inclusion of different currencies (87.5%) in a global EIS is considered to be an important feature by a majority of the respondents. Since most of the time senior executives examine and evaluate financial data in an organization it becomes important to include different currencies. The ability to convert from different currencies to dollars and make comparisons of sales worldwide will assist executives in making better decisions.

A system that is developed for executives working in a global organization must include multi-lingual capabilities for greater acceptance. The results show that three-fourths of the respondents (75.0%) are of the opinion that a global EIS should incorporate multi-lingual capabilities. Not only does it become easier for executives worldwide to use a system with multi-lingual capabilities, it also would encourage executives to use it more frequently.

Executives are more concerned primarily with financial data, and quantities of units sold in different measurement units may not be as important for senior executives. This explains the fact that not too many respondents consider inclusion of different measurement units (68.7%) to be equally important. The fact that there are only two main measurement systems used in most parts of the world might also explain the opinions of the respondents.

THE NATIONAL ENVIRONMENT

Q. What are the different external sources of information that can be used for a global executive information system?

Proposition: The greater the intensity of the global competition that an organization faces, in its national environment (home country), the greater will be the demand for external sources of information for a global EIS.

Proposition: The greater the governmental constraints imposed on the acquisition of information by organizations (in home country), the less likely it is that the quality of information in a global EIS would be effective/good.

Proposition : The greater the level of uncertainty in the national environment of an organization, the greater will be the demand for external information for a global EIS.

The environmental forces in the national environment (home country) of an organization create the need for information for a global organization. This organizational need for information is fulfilled by collecting and analyzing information from different sources that are available to an organization in its national environment. Based on the literature and case study results, nine types of information sources were identified as potentially relevant for obtaining international business information within the national environment of a company. As information can and is usually obtained from multiple sources, respondents were allowed to check multiple sources. The percent frequency of use of each information source is shown in the Table 3.

Table 3 Sources of information and their percent frequency use

Source	Percent frequency
Online databases	83.3
Suppliers/customers/trade associations	66.7
Published (trade/general/govt. pubs.)	64.6
Academic institutions/private research labs.	58.3
Information brokers/consultants	54.2
Chambers of commerce	35.4
Conferences/trade-shows	35.4
Business travels	31.3
Personal contacts	31.3

The highest recommended source of information used by companies for gathering international information in the opinion of the respondents is on-line databases. Other sources that are considered important are suppliers/customers/trade associations; published (trade/general/government publications); academic institutions/private research labs.; and information brokers and consultants. It is apparent that most of the widely preferred sources of information are hard sources of information. The "explosive growth" of the Internet in recent years is an indicator of the popularity of such sources of information and the preference for such information. Not only is information more readily available, it is also more easy to access, and to a great extent accurate and reliable. A possible reason for a low use of chambers of commerce and conferences/trade shows as sources of information is the fact that these sources are confined to the gathering and collecting information pertaining to the local environment, rather than international information. While personal contacts and travels do provide invaluable insights, a high reliance on these sources is not desirable as is shown by the results.

The demand for international information required for a global EIS varies with the level of global competition that an organization faces in its home country. The survey findings reveal that 72.9 % of the respondents believe that the intensity of the global competition that an organization faces directly impacts the demand for external sources of information for a global EIS. Every company that is faced with global competition will be trying to look for more information on its competition. Executive information systems developed during the 80s were a direct result of the need for such information within the context of local competition. With increasing globalization the demand for external sources of international business information has become greater.

Another factor that impacts the demand for international information for a global EIS is the level of uncertainty in the environment. Three-fourths (75.1%) of the respondents agree that the greater the level of uncertainty in the national environment of an organization, the greater will be the demand for external information for a global EIS. Most of the global corporations in the United States operate in a very dynamic environment. This increases the uncertainty in the environment leading to a greater demand for information on global competitors.

The quality of the information that is used in a global EIS will be affected by the constraints that are imposed by the government, on the acquisition of such information. The results of the study show that only 58.3% of the people believe that government constraints on the acquisition of information, impacts the quality of the information that is used in a global EIS. United States is a country where there are very few constraints on acquisition of information by companies. Information is freely available to anyone who wants to use it, especially with the growth of the Internet. The free access to information can be a possible explanation for the low response.

ORGANIZATIONAL ENVIRONMENT

Q. How does the usage of a global executive information system impact the organization?

Proposition: The effectiveness of the global EIS in a global organization will be greater if the global EIS supports the overall organizational strategy (Ives & Jarvenpaa, 1991).

Proposition: The value of global EIS investments for a global organization will increase with the diffusion of the system.

The literature review and case study results pointed out that the usage of a global EIS impacts the organization in the following ways: increases individual and organizational learning, decreases the frequency and duration of executive meetings, decreases the number of organizational levels involved in decision-making, increases confidence in decision-making, leads to an increase in organizational scanning of internal and external environments, decreases involvement of subordinates in analysis.

Respondents were asked to indicate their opinion about the impact on an organization of using a global EIS. The percent frequency of each of the impact factors is shown in Table 4. A vast majority of the respondents agree that the usage of a global EIS in an organization leads to an increase in the confidence of decision making. This indicates that with access to greater amounts of relevant information, executives feel more confidant in their decision-making. It also explains why approximately two thirds of the respondents agree that use of a global EIS will lead to an increase in organizational scanning of internal and external environments of a company. To satisfy the need of executives for more international information to be used in a global EIS, an organization will have to scan more sources of internal and external information. More than three-fourths of the respondents also agree that with greater information available to executives in a global organization, individual and organizational learning will increase. It is evident that this increase in learning is a consequence of the availability of more information in an organization that can be used by executives in their decision-making process.

Table 4 Impact of usage of a GEIS in an organization

Impact	Agree/ strongly agree%	Neither agree or disagree %	Disagree/ strongly disagree %
Increases confidence in decision-making	87.6	10.4	2.0
Increases individual and organizational learning	81.2	10.4	8.4
Leads to increase in organizational scanning of internal and external environments	68.8	29.2	2.0
Decreases the number of organizational levels involved in decision-making	31.3	33.3	35.4
Decreases involvement of subordinates in analysis	23.0	22.9	54.1
Decreases frequency and duration of executive meetings	18.8	43.8	37.4

The results show that slightly less than one-thirds of the respondents agree that the use of a global EIS will lead to a decrease in the organizational levels involved in decision-making. Further less than one-fourth of the respondents agree that the use of a global EIS will lead to a decrease in the involvement of subordinates in analysis, or a decrease in the frequency and duration of executive meetings. These results point out that even though the confidence of executives in decision-making is higher with the use of a global EIS, it does not necessarily impact the organizational structure and processes used for decision making. A possible explanation could be the fact that it would take more time before executives feel comfortable with relying primarily on a global EIS for decision-making. A change in their work style, for example less reliance on subordinates for analysis etc., would take time. Also meetings for executives are a source of both information gathering and a social process. A decrease in the number of meetings impacts the social aspect of the work of an executive and may not be welcome by executives. This explains the fact that respondents do not agree that the use of a global EIS will lead to a decrease in the frequency and duration of executive meetings.

As mentioned earlier, the confidence in decision making increases with the use of a global EIS. It is important to mention here that for confidence to increase, a global EIS should support the overall organizational strategy. A majority of the respondents (91.7%) agree that a global EIS that supports the overall organizational strategy will be more effective and the result is consistent with the literature (Buss, 1982; Ives & Jarvenpaa, 1991; Reck, 1989). Respondents also agree (79.2%) that greater value will be derived from the use of a global EIS in an organization, if the system is used by a large number of executives.

GEIS USER ENVIRONMENT

Q. What should be the scope of the global executive information system?

Q. Who are the primary users of the global executive information system?

Proposition: Initiation of the global EIS project by business executives (functional heads or CEO, rather than IS personnel) will increase the chances of success of the system (global EIS).

Proposition: The higher the organizational level of the initiator of the global EIS project, the better the chances of its being successful. (Watson et al., 1991)

Proposition: The higher the organizational level of executive sponsorship, the greater is the degree of success of the global EIS. (Watson et al., 1991)

Proposition: The higher the organizational level of operating sponsorship, the greater is the degree of success of the global EIS. (Watson et al., 1991)

The user environment identifies the scope of the global EIS that is used in an organization, the people who are the primary users of the system, and the people who should be involved in providing direction for its development. Case study results were used to identify four broad categories of "scope" for a global EIS. The four categories developed for the scope of a global EIS are: the global organization (enterprise wide); regional organization (e.g., European subsidiaries, Asia-Pacific subsidiaries etc.); product division (the entire organization for a product line); and department/function (the entire organization for one department or function). Respondents were asked to check only one category. In case respondents did not agree with any of these categories they were allowed the option of identifying any "other" category. Table 5 shows the frequency percentage of the different categories.

More than three-fourths of the respondents were of the opinion that the scope of the global EIS should be enterprise-wide, i.e., the global organization. Very few respondents recommended the regional organization (12.5%), product division (6.3%) or the department/function (2.0%) as the scope for a global EIS. Watson et al. (1991) talk about the existence of some EIS that are developed for functional areas in a business. We can make the conclusion that majority of the EIS are developed for the entire organization, which is consistent with the results of this study.

Table 5: Scope of the Global EIS

Scope	Frequency percentage
Global organization	79.2
Regional organization	12.5
Product division	6.3
Department / function	2.0

When asked to identify the primary users of a global EIS, the categories specified included CEO (headquarters); top management (subsidiaries only); top management (headquarters only); middle management (subsidiaries only); and middle management (headquarters only). Respondents were asked to select all the categories of users that they thought were important. In case respondents did not agree with these categories they could include "others" as their choice. Table 6 provides a frequency percentage listing of the choices made.

Table 6: Primary users of a Global EIS

Primary users	Frequency percentage
Top management (headquarters only)	97.9
Top management (subs. only)	89.6
CEO (headquarters)	81.3
Middle management (headquarters only)	64.6
Middle management (subsidiaries only)	60.4

Majority of the respondents recommended that the CEO and top management at headquarters and subsidiaries of a global organization should be primary users. There is not overwhelming support for including middle management at headquarters or in subsidiaries as primary users of a global EIS. This is in comparison to the results for including senior management as primary users of the system. As a global EIS is designed specifically for senior executives working in a global organization, the results are reinforcing. Middle management if included as primary users of the system would create the need for additional capabilities (DeLong & Rockart, 1992) to be provided in a global EIS. These capabilities are based on specific job functions, work styles and support needs of middle management in an organization.

It is interesting to note that respondents feel that senior management in subsidiaries should be included as primary users of the system. This will benefit the entire organization as decision-making will be facilitated across the organization. Some of the respondents who included "others" in their choice offered the following comments: 'external customers (business partners) may also want/need access'; 'professionals, e.g., engineers, research scientists etc.'; and 'strategic planners, financial analysts, marketing. . . .'

When asked about the initiator of the global EIS project, two-thirds of the respondents (66.6%) agreed that business executives (at hdqrs.. and subs.) rather than IS personnel should initiate the global EIS project. This result is consistent with the literature (Houdshel & Watson, 1987; Stecklow, 1989) that business executives should be the initiators of the EIS project. The Watson et al. (1991) study had reported a surprising finding when they said that more IS departments are taking the lead in initiating EIS development. This could possibly explain the 25% response of those people who do not disagree or agree. Respondents (83.3%) also agreed that the higher the organizational level of the initiator of the global EIS project, the better the chances of success of the project. This result is consistent with the literature (Barrow, 1990; Rockart & DeLong, 1988) which says that a highly placed senior executive initiates an EIS project.

Watson et al. (1991) and Rockart and DeLong (1988) point out that the executive sponsor (one who provides direction for system development) and the operating sponsor (one who manages day-to-day development) for an EIS are senior executives in an organization. When asked about the organizational level of the sponsors, more than two-thirds of the respondents agreed that the higher the organizational level of the executive sponsor and the operating sponsor of the global EIS project, the better the chances of success of the project. These results point out that the primary users of a global EIS (executives) should be involved actively in the initiation and sponsorship of the global EIS project to ensure successful implementation.

GEIS DEVELOPMENT ENVIRONMENT

Q. Who is responsible for planning the development of the global executive information system?

Q. What methodology should be used to determine and validate information requirements for a global executive information system?

Q. What methodology should be used to develop a global executive information system?

Q. How should the global executive information system be developed (in-house vs customization of off the shelf software product)?

Q. Who should develop the global executive information system? Where should the system be developed?

Q. What are the skills required of members on the global EIS development team?

In the global EIS development environment an attempt is made to identify the person(s) responsible for planning the development of a global EIS, methodologies used for determining information requirements and for developing a global EIS, the approaches for developing a global EIS, the people who should be on the development team, the skills required of members on the development team, and the number of people who should be there on the development team.

When asked as to who should be responsible for planning the development of the global EIS, the following five choices were provided: initiator of the global EIS project, executive sponsor, operating sponsor, CIO, and steering committee. An "others" option was provided for respondents who wanted to include any other person. Table 7 shows the frequency percentage for the different people responsible for planning the development of a global EIS.

Table 7: Person(s) responsible for planning the global EIS

Person(s)	Percent frequency
Steering committee	33.3
CIO (chief information officer)	27.1
Executive sponsor	16.7
Operating sponsor	14.5
Initiator of the GEIS project	6.3
Others	2.1

One-thirds of the respondents felt that a steering committee should be made responsible for planning the global EIS project. This result indicates that respondents do not want any one person to be made responsible for planning the project. It also agrees with Buss's (1982) recommendation that an "international computer council" be created to develop plans for global information systems and to ensure that they are compatible with corporate plans. This group of people drawn from different parts of the world would be able to provide better direction for the project. It would also provide a sense of ownership for people working in subsidiaries.

The instrument identified five different methodologies for determining and validating information requirements for a global EIS. The methodologies identified include: asking executives, critical success factors, prototyping, ends means analysis, and deriving from an existing application. Respondents were allowed to select any number of methodologies from this list. In case they felt that this list was not comprehensive, they were allowed to mention "others" as their choice along with an explanation. Table 8 provides frequency percentages of the methodologies preferred by respondents for determining information requirements.

Table 8: Methodologies for determining and validating information requirements of a Global EIS

Methodologies	Percent frequency
Asking executives	81.3
Critical success factors	79.2
Prototyping	77.1
Deriving from an existing application	41.7
Ends-means analysis	33.3

It should be pointed out here that a working definition of critical success factors, prototyping, and ends means analysis was provided in the instrument. The three methodologies perceived to be important by respondents are asking executives, critical success factors, and prototyping. Asking executives directly for the information they need or the use of critical success factors for an executives work environment can be used to come up with a conceptual understanding or framework of information required by executives. Care must be taken to see how executives are asked for their information requirements. Prototyping can then be used for determining the detailed requirements of the system. This explains the respondents' choice of selecting these three methodologies. The methodologies selected by respondents agree with the literature (Watson & Frolick, 1992; Wetherbe, 1991). It is interesting to note here that respondents selected methodologies which not only assist developers to draw a conceptual framework, but also to determine details required for a global EIS. Some of the respondents who choose "others" as one of their choices mentioned the following methodologies: 'bench marking, brainstorming, joint requirements determination, information analysis, and work process'. No explanations were however provided for including these methodologies.

The results of the case studies and literature review analysis resulted in identifying six methodologies for developing a global EIS. The methodologies are SDLC, structured methodologies, data modeling, information engineering, joint application development, and prototyping. There was an "others" category provided for respondents who wanted to include a new development methodology. Respondents were asked to check all the methodologies that they considered important. Table 9 provides the frequency percentage of the methodologies selected by respondents.

Table 9: Development methodologies for a global EIS

Development methodologies	Percent frequency
Prototyping	66.7
Joint application development	62.5
Data modeling	58.3
Information engineering	45.8
SDLC	41.7
Structured methodologies	41.7

The choice of prototyping as the most popular methodology highlights the fact that the time taken for developing a global EIS is an important factor. Other reasons that can possibly explain the respondents' choice, may be the unstructured nature of information required for decision-making in an executive's work environment and the difficulty of determining information requirements. Prototyping provides executives a chance to preview the results of the system from time to time and recommend any changes that they feel should be incorporated. This result also agrees with the literature (Moad, 1988; Rainer & Watson, 1995; Runge, 1988). Joint application development (62.5%) provides an opportunity for developers and users to work together during the development process. This ensures to a great extent that the system that is finally developed meets the users requirements (Wetherbe, 1991). It explains the respondents preference for this methodology. Other methodologies selected by respondents were not considered very important for developing a global EIS.

For developing the global EIS four different approaches were identified. They are in-house development, customization of off-the-shelf software, a combination of both, and using off-the-shelf software. In case respondents wanted to add another category, they were allowed to include it under the "other" category. Table 10 provides the results for the different approaches for developing a global EIS.

Table 10: Approaches for developing a Global EIS

Approaches	Frequency percent
Combination of in-house development and off-the-shelf software customization	58.3
Customization of off-the-shelf software	16.7
In-house development	10.4
Off-the-shelf software	8.3
Other	6.3

More than half of the respondents thought that a combination of in-house development and customization of off-the-shelf software is the most appropriate approach for developing a global EIS (Rockart & Delong, 1988; Watson et al., 1991). The result is not surprising, as there are several vendors in the market who provide an EIS for an organization. Customization of the EIS product to include the international dimension would enable an organization to have a system in place in a short time frame. This would be supported by executives as they get to use the system early on. Changes if required can then be incorporated as desired by the executives.

Three choices were provided for determining the composition of the global EIS development team. Majority of the respondents (83.3%) felt that cross-national teams (i.e., combination of hdqrs. and subsidiary employees) would be the best combination of people for developing the system. This is important in view of the fact that users in subsidiaries will feel an ownership of the system if they are involved in its development (Buss, 1982). Also the usage of the system in subsidiaries would increase if people from subsidiaries are involved.

When asked to identify the number of people that should be there on the development team, respondents were allowed to check any one option from the following table.

Table 11: Number of people on the Global EIS development team

Number of people	Percent frequency
0–5	25.0
6–10	58.3
11–15	12.5
16 and more	4.2

More than half of the respondents believed that 6–10 people is the ideal size for a cross-national team of developers. This is a group size, which is both manageable and can include people from different functional areas and nations. The literature points out that on an average four people (Watson et al., 1991) should be there on the EIS development team. Since a global EIS development team would need to include people from other countries, a team size of 6–10 people would be ideal.

Six different skills were identified for potential members of the development team. The skills are business area knowledge, interpersonal skills, IS (technical skills), cultural (language skills), data knowledge and executive perspective. An "others" category was also included for respondents to identify a new skill. The results are presented in Table 12.

It is interesting to observe that business area knowledge was rated higher than IS technical skills. This highlights the fact that it is important for global EIS developers to have an excellent understanding of the functional areas of the business and also the job environment of an executive (Watson et al., 1991). Respondents also considered interpersonal skills, an executive perspective and data knowledge as important desirable skills. Surprisingly, familiarity with a foreign language was not considered important in view of the fact that majority of the respondents favored a cross-national team of developers. A possible explanation can be the fact that most IS trained people or other members of the team would have an understanding and working knowledge of the English language.

Table 12: Global EIS development team skills required

Skills	Percent frequency
Business area knowledge	95.8
IS (technical skills)	75.0
Interpersonal skills	70.8
Executive perspective	68.8
Data knowledge	68.8
Cultural (language) skills	45.8

Five different categories of people were identified as potential members on the global EIS development team. These categories are executives, executive staff, business analyst, systems analysts, and programmers. Respondents were asked to identify the single most important category of people who should be there on the global EIS development team (Table 13).

Table 13: Composition of Global EIS development team

Type of people	Percent frequency
Business analyst	40
Executives (top management)	37
Systems analysts	15
Executive staff	6
Programmers	2

The results show that emphasis is placed on including people with business skills, rather that technical skills. It highlights the fact that respondents believe that if information requirements for a global EIS can be determined, developing the system (coding or customization) would not be too much of a problem. These results reinforce the fact that knowledge of the business environment is more important than programming for developing a global EIS (Watson et al., 1991).

GLOBAL EIS OPERATIONS ENVIRONMENT

Q. What should be the hardware configuration for using a global executive information system?

Q. Where does a global company operate information processing centers for effective transmission of data?

Proposition: Standardized distributed databases are more appropriate for a global EIS.

Proposition: A customized global EIS (software) for executives in different parts of the world will lead to greater acceptance of the system.

Proposition: The greater the extent of documentation of the global EIS, the easier it will be to maintain the system.

Proposition: Localized (in subsidiaries) support staff (both technical and data entry) is essential for a global EIS.

The global EIS environment is used for identifying the resources, hardware, software, databases, procedures and documentation, processing centers etc., required to operate the global EIS. Respondents were asked to choose the most effective hardware configuration from the following: centralized (mainframe/minicomputer based); decentralized (minicomputer/PCS/LANs) or distributed (enterprise wide networks/WANs using workstations). Table 14 shows the preferences of respondents for the most effective hardware configuration for a global EIS.

Two-thirds of the respondents feel that a distributed hardware configuration would be the most effective for a global EIS. This is a fitting response as it highlights the fact that respondents want executives in subsidiaries to be using the global EIS. In the Watson et al. (1991) study the hardware configuration that was most desirable for an EIS was the mainframe approach (shared mainframe and a PC network connected to a mainframe). Volonino, Watson, and Robinson (1995) recommend using networked workstations for an EIS. The results of this study are consistent with the literature keeping in mind the fact that the recommended hardware configuration is for a system that would be used worldwide.

Table 14: Hardware configuration for a global EIS

Configuration	Percent frequency
Distributed	67
Decentralized	15
Centralized	12
Others	6

When asked where should the processing center(s) for a global EIS be located, respondents were provided with three choices: headquarters only, regional (e.g., European) processing centers, and/or country (subsidiaries) processing centers. The results are provided in Table 15.

This is a surprising result in view of the fact that respondents preferred an enterprise wide network for hardware configuration. A possible explanation can be the fact that respondents want data to be collected from different offices worldwide using an enterprise wide system, but processed and analyzed at the headquarters. The information can then be distributed over the different regional and country centers in a global organization.

Table 15: Global EIS processing center(s)

Location	Percent frequency
Headquarters only	52.1
Regional centers	43.8
Country processing centers	22.9

When asked about the databases to be used for a global EIS, respondents agree (60.4%) that distributed databases are more appropriate for a global EIS. Only 4.2% of the respondents disagreed. Providing access to data worldwide for senior executives so that they can preview and process data is important. As distributed configuration was the choice of respondents for the hardware configuration, this result is not surprising.

Three-fourths of the respondents (75.0%) agree that customization of the global EIS software for executives worldwide will lead to greater acceptance among users. Only 4.2% of the respondents disagreed. This is consistent with the literature (Rockart & DeLong, 1988; Watson et al., 1991) which points out that an EIS should be customized for its executive users. Two-thirds (66.6%) of the respondents agree that the greater the documentation provided for the global EIS, the easier will it be to maintain the system. The need for support staff at different locations worldwide is greatly reduced if there is adequate documentation provided. The results show that 60.3% of the respondents agree that providing localized support staff in subsidiaries will lead to greater usage.

CHAPTER 4

The Global EIS Use, Development and Operations Process

THE GLOBAL EIS USE PROCESS

Q. How does the use of a global EIS impact the work of an executive?

Proposition: The greater the quality of the decision-making is, resulting from the usage of the global EIS by executives, the greater will be the satisfaction of executives.

The global EIS use process measures the impact of using a global EIS, on the work of an executive and satisfaction resulting from the usage of the system. The literature review and case study results identified three major impacts as a result of using a global EIS: improved quality of decision making, improved productivity in decision making and faster task completion. Table 16 presents the results of the impact of using a global EIS on the work of an executive.

Table 16: Impact of using a Global EIS on Executive work

Impact	Yes	No
Improved quality of decision-making	95.8%	4.2%
Improved productivity in decision-making	70.8%	29.2%
Faster task completion (leads to faster implementation of a decision)	27.1%	72.9%

As the table indicates an overwhelming majority of the respondents believe that the use of a global EIS results in an improvement in the quality of decision-making. More than two-thirds respondents also believe that the usage of a global EIS results in improved productivity in the decision-making process. The results clearly show that access to timely information (external and internal) leads to an improvement in the decision-making process and the quality of decisions made.

Respondents (72.9%) do not believe that the usage of a global EIS results in faster task completion for executives. The result is different from what the literature indicates (Elam & Leidner, 1995; Rainer & Watson, 1995; Watson et al., 1993). In an earlier section it was shown that the use of a global EIS by executives does not lead to a decrease in the involvement of subordinates for analysis of information. The need for detailed analysis of information by executives may lead to more time being spent before the final decision is made. Also the fact that international information is being analyzed can impact the time that is taken for analysis. This could be a possible explanation for the respondents' viewpoint.

GLOBAL EIS DEVELOPMENT PROCESS

Proposition: Active participation by executives (primary users) in the development process of the global EIS will lead to a better quality system being developed.

Proposition: Active participation by secondary users (operations and maintenance personnel) in the development process of the global EIS will lead to a better quality system being developed.

Proposition: Active participation by executives in the development process of the global EIS will lead to greater satisfaction with the system (in turn increasing the chances of success of the system).

Proposition: Active participation by executives in the development process will ensure adequate funding for the project.

Q. What are the costs associated with the development of a global EIS?

Proposition: The benefits of using a global EIS will justify the cost spend on developing the global EIS. (Watson et al. 1991)

Q. What is the time taken to develop the global EIS?

The development process is measured in terms of the extent of participation of the users in the development of the system. Table 17 presents the results of the respondents.

Table 17: Impact of active participation by users on the system

Impact	Strongly disagree/ disagree	Neither agree or disagree	Strongly agree/ agree
Active participation by primary users leads to a better quality system	2.1	6.3	91.6
Active participation by primary users leads to greater satisfaction being derived from the system	2.1	6.3	91.6
Active participation by secondary users leads to a better quality system being developed	4.2	25.0	70.8

As is evident from the table an overwhelming majority of the respondents believe that active participation by primary users (executives) in the development process will lead to a better quality system being developed. More than three-fourths of the respondents also believe that active participation by secondary users will lead to a better quality system being developed. This result is consistent with the literature (Wetherbe, 1991) where it is mentioned that it is important to include users in the development process.

If users are actively involved in the development process, the output of the system will lead to greater satisfaction for executives (Wetherbe, 1991). Providing access to information needed by executives will not only lead to greater satisfaction, but will ensure adequate funding for the project (62.5%) as pointed out by respondents. Only 12.5% of the respondents disagree.

Watson et al. (1991) point out that companies "consider the costs involved before undertaking EIS development". In this study the respondents were asked to provide cost estimates for developing and operating a global EIS. Respondents (N = 26) believe that the average cost of developing a global EIS is $7.7 million approximately. The median cost for these respondents is $875,000 (Figure 3). Of this total cost for developing a global EIS, respondents (N = 28) allocated 35% for hardware, 48% for software, and 17% for training purposes. The average cost of developing a global EIS ($7.7 million) is significantly higher than the cost of developing an EIS, which is $365,000 on an average (Watson et al., 1991).

The average operating cost for a global EIS is $784,423.08. The median cost for operating a global EIS is $147,500 (Figure 4). Respondents (N = 18) allocated 36% for hardware, 48% for software, and 16% for training. The average cost of operating a global EIS ($784,423.08) is significantly higher than the cost of operating an EIS, which is $208,000 on an average (Watson et al., 1991). As is evident from these results the cost of developing and operating a global EIS is very high. This leads us to believe that such systems will be limited to the larger global corporations similar to the case of EIS (Watson et al., 1991).

When asked that the benefits of using a global EIS will justify the cost spend on developing the global EIS, 52.0% of the respondents agreed and only 4.2% of the respondents replied in the negative. The difficulty of quantifying benefits (Houdshel & Watson, 1987; Moad, 1988; Rockart & DeLong, 1988; Rockart & Treacy, 1982; Watson et al., 1991) is a possible explanation for this response. We can draw the conclusion that improvements in decision-making for the executive, due to global EIS usage, will eventually justify the cost spend on developing the system. The benefits that are derived as a result of using the system are intangible rather than tangible.

Table 18 depicts the respondents' opinions with respect to the time that should be taken to develop a global EIS.

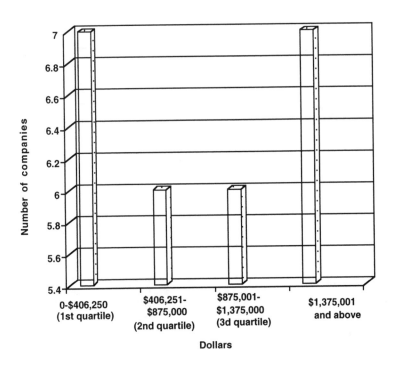

Figure 3: Development Cost (N = 26)

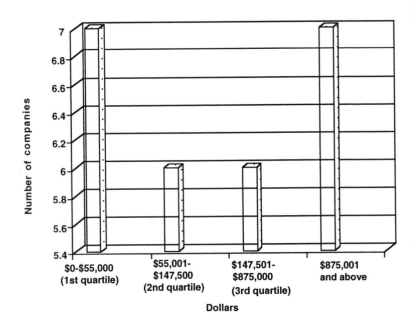

Figure 4: Operating Cost (N = 26)

Table 18: Time taken to develop a Global EIS

Time taken (in months)	Frequency percent
0–3	6.2
3–6	27.1
6–12	47.9
12–24	18.8

As the table indicates majority of the respondents want a global EIS to be developed within a year's time frame. A six-to-twelve month is the recommended time for the system development process. Moad (1988) and Runge (1988) point out that an initial version of an EIS should be developed quickly to enable executives to provide feedback on the system. The results of this study reinforce the fact that a shorter time frame is best suited for developing a global executive information system.

GLOBAL EIS OPERATIONS PROCESS

Proposition: High error rates (inaccurate information etc.) in the usage of the global EIS will lead to dissatisfied users.

Proposition: The greater the flexibility of the global EIS to incorporate changing requirements, the greater will be the satisfaction of the users. (Rainer & Watson, 1995; Watson et al., 1993; Wetherbe, 1991)

Proposition: An increase in the number of executive users of a global EIS will lead to better chances of success for the global EIS. (Friend, 1990; Watson et al., 1991)

Proposition: An increase in the number of executive users of a global EIS will lead to an increase in the number of screens (more information) demanded by executives. (Watson et al. 1991)

The operation process measures the physical operation of the system. Table 19 presents the results of the global EIS process variables, for the propositions listed above.

Table 19: Global EIS process variables

Process variables	Strongly disagree/disagree	Neither agree or disagree	Strongly agree/agree
Increase in executive users of a GEIS leads to better chances of success for the system	2.1	8.3	89.6
Flexible GEIS leads to satisfied users	2.1	22.9	75.0
Increased demand for screens due to increased executive users	10.4	14.6	75.0
High error rates will lead to dissatisfied users	35.4	22.9	41.7

As the table indicates, majority of the respondents agree that an operational global EIS, which is initially successful, will lead to an increase in the number of executive users. This will in turn lead to better chances of success for the global EIS. This result strengthens Friends (1990) argument that an EIS that does not spread is likely to fail. It must be noted here that the if the spread of a global EIS is among non-executives, additional capabilities will be demanded (Rockart & DeLong, 1988) by users.

Three-fourths of the respondents agree that the flexibility of a global EIS is essential for acceptance of the system by users. Failure to incorporate changing requirements or meeting needs of executives will lead to a failure of the system (Wetherbe, 1991). This result also reinforces Rainer and Watson's (1995) contention that adapting to changing information requirements is a key operational EIS factor.

Three-fourths of the respondents agree that an operational global EIS which is initially successful will lead to an increased demand for the number of screens by executives. This result is consistent with the Watson et al. (1991) study.

Only 41.7% of the respondents agree that obvious small to moderate error rates in the global EIS will not impact the usefulness of the system. This implies that respondents believe that the reliability of the system is very important. High error rates due to inaccurate information can lead to dissatisfied users and this result is consistent with the Rainer and Watson (1995) study.

CHAPTER 5

The Global EIS Architecture

The global EIS architecture shows the different components of the final system that is developed for executives in a global organization. The following paragraphs present and discuss the results for the different components of the global EIS system.

GLOBAL EIS DATA MANAGEMENT

Q. What is the scope of the data that is to be included in a global EIS?

Q. What are the potential problems in a global EIS with respect to data management?

Proposition: Inclusion of soft data in the global EIS will improve the quality of the global EIS (Mintzberg, 1975; Watson et al., 1991; Zmud, 1986).

The literature (Houdshel & Watson, 1987; Rockart & DeLong, 1988; Watson et al.,1991) points out that data is a very important part of an EIS, as it forms the basis of the information that is provided to executives by the EIS. The question that arises in the case of a global EIS is the scope of the data that should be included in a global EIS and the potential problems with respect to managing this data. In an earlier section it was reported that 79.2% of the respondents were of the opinion that the scope of the global EIS should be the global organization. Majority of the respondents (91.6%) felt that the scope of the data that is included in a global EIS should be the global organization. This data is internal to the organization and would be extracted from databases that exist in the organization, e.g., transaction processing systems and functional areas (Watson et al., 1991).

All respondents agree that data integrity (100%), data security (100%), and data standards (100%) are important issues for the management of data that is used for generating information for a global EIS.

Mintzberg (1975) and Zmud (1986) point out the significance of internal data that is captured from human sources and that it is very important to understand complex problems. Watson et al. (1991) define this as "soft-data" and include news, rumors, opinions, ideas, predictions, explanations, and plans in this category of data. In their opinion capturing this data as a part of an EIS can be a difficult process. They however point out that this data will add to the "richness" of the information that is provided by an EIS. Respondents (73.0%) agree that it is important to include soft data in a global EIS and that the inclusion of such data in the global EIS will lead to a better quality system being developed. Table 20 shows the results for the different data management issues.

Table 20: Data management issues for a Global EIS

Data management issues	Not important	Of little importance	Somewhat important	Important	Very important
Data integrity	-	-	-	27.1	72.9
Data security	-	-	12.5	25.0	62.5
Data standards	-	-	20.8	50.0	29.2
Inclusion of soft data	2.0	25.0	56.3	14.6	2.1

GLOBAL EIS KNOWLEDGE MANAGEMENT

Proposition: Inclusion of executive expertise in the global EIS will enhance the quality of the system. (Eom, 1994; Min & Eom, 1994; Turban, 1995)

Min and Eom (1994) point out that a knowledge base bridges the gap between information provided by using quantitative analysis models and reality. As a result of this executives may face problems in solving complex and unstructured problems. Majority of the respondents (85.5%) felt that the inclusion of such a knowledge base will enhance the quality of the global EIS that is developed. This knowledge will be useful for solving complex problems in the global business environment and would also provide an explanation for some of the solutions.

GLOBAL EIS MODEL MANAGEMENT

Proposition: A model base incorporated in the global EIS will increase the effectiveness of the system. (Eom, 1994; Min & Eom, 1994; Turban, 1995)

Including quantitative and analytical models in systems that are developed for executives has been recommended by several researchers (Eom, 1994; Min & Eom, 1994; Turban, 1995). In this study, a majority of the respondents (93.8%) were of the opinion that the inclusion of a model management in a global EIS is important. The respondents believe that such a component will increase the effectiveness of the system that is developed. This is a significant result as it shows a preference for analysis and modeling capabilities in a global EIS. Executives need to evaluate alternatives and conduct "what-if" and sensitivity analysis in their decision-making process.

GLOBAL EIS PRESENTATION FORMAT

Proposition: Customization of the global EIS for individual users (e.g. executives in different parts of the world) in a global organization will lead to greater usage of the system.

Q. What are the features that are required to present information to executives using a global EIS?

Watson et al. (1991) point out that the ease with which the executives can use a system developed for them is very important. All the respondents (100%) in this study were of the opinion that the ease of use of a global EIS is an important issue. If executives have to be trained for more than a few minutes to use the system then it will not satisfy the executives.

Information that is generated by an EIS should be presented to executives in different formats, for example tables, graphs, text etc. (Friend, 1988; Houdshel & Watson, 1987; Rockart & DeLong, 1988; Watson et al., 1991). All the respondents (100%) were of the opinion that the information should be presented to the executives in a desired format, 95.8% of the respondents recommended the use of graphics for presenting information, and 93.7% of the respondents recommended using color for presenting information to the executives. These results point out that executives should be provided information by a global EIS in different formats and the use of graphs and color is highly desirable.

Providing electronic mail as a capability for information presentation in an EIS is mentioned in the literature (Jordan, 1993; Watson et al., 1991). In this study, 79.2% of the respondents were of the opinion that incorporating electronic mail capabilities in a global EIS is important. The electronic mail capability would allow executives to communicate with other people from anywhere at any time. This is very important in a global organization as it reduces the need to meet people from different subsidiaries from time-to-time.

Rockart and DeLong (1988) indicate using electronic calendars in an EIS as an organizing tool for executives. 60.4% of the respondents in this study were of the opinion that a "scheduler" for appointments was of importance to them. This would allow executives to keep track of their appointments, especially when they are travelling. Table 21 shows the results of the features desired for information presentation in a global EIS.

Table 21: Desired features for information presentation in a Global EIS

Information presentation features	Not important	Of little importance	Somewhat important	Important	Very important
Ease of use	-	-	-	33.3	66.7
Information presentation in a format desired by executives	-	-	10.4	50.0	39.6
Use of graphics	-	4.2	18.8	52.1	25.0
Use of color	-	6.3	25.0	47.9	20.8
E-mail package	10.4	10.4	14.6	35.4	29.2
Scheduler (appointments)	25.0	14.6	33.3	20.8	6.3

GLOBAL EIS USER-INTERFACE

Proposition: Menus and icons will be preferred by executives over command languages in a global EIS. (Watson et al., 1991)

Proposition: A global EIS with slow response time will lead to dissatisfied executive users. (Houdshel & Watson, 1987; Rockart & DeLong, 1988; Watson et al., 1991)

Zmud (1986) points out that the executive considers the dialog with the EIS to be the most important part of the system. It becomes important to ensure that information is provided to an executive with minimal delay. The significance of the response time in an EIS is highlighted by Watson et al. (1991), Rockart and DeLong (1988), and Houdshel and Watson (1987). All the respondents (100%) in this study agree that a global EIS with slow response time will lead to dissatisfied users.

Executives should not have to use the keyboard to interact with the system for using a global EIS. Watson et al. (1991) point out that some executives may be adverse to using the keyboard and alternatives can be provided for such executives. In this study, 97.9% of the respondents were of the opinion that there should be a minimum number of keystrokes required to use the global EIS. Respondents considered the use of menus/icons (100%) and mouse/touch screens (97.9%) to be important for interacting with the system. Table 22 presents the results of the global EIS user-interface component of the system.

Table 22: User-Interface component features for a Global EIS

Features	Not important	Of little importance	Somewhat important	Important	Very important
On-line	-	-	18.8	41.7	39.6
Menus/icons	-	-	20.8	47.9	31.3
Minimum # of keystrokes	-	2.1	25.0	37.5	35.4
Mouse/touch screen	-	2.1	29.2	39.6	29.2

REASONS FOR DEVELOPING A GLOBAL EIS AND POTENTIAL PROBLEMS

The literature review and case study results were used to identify several reasons why global organizations develop a global EIS and the potential problems that can be faced during the development of the system. Table 23 shows the results for the reasons for developing a global EIS.

Table 23: Reasons for developing a Global EIS

Reasons	Yes	No
Increases quality of decision-making	97.9	2.1
Useful for making strategic decisions	85.4	14.6
Provides organization with competitive advantage	77.1	22.9
Access to unavailable information	60.4	39.6

Increase in the quality of decision-making, the usefulness of a global EIS for making strategic decisions, and providing organizations with competitive advantages are perceived to be important factors for developing a global EIS. Surprisingly, access to unavailable information is not considered to be a very important reason for developing a global EIS. It is possible that respondents feel that information can be made accessible for executives, but the problem lies in putting it together and providing it in a system that can be used easily by executives. Table 24 highlights some potential problems for developing a global EIS.

Table 24: *Problems in developing a Global EIS*

Problems	Yes	No
Defining the objectives of the system	81.3	18.2
Determining the information requirements of the system	79.2	20.8
Getting executives to use the system	58.3	41.7
Determining hardware and software required for system	25.0	75.0
Regional IT support in subsidiaries	20.8	79.2

Defining the objectives of the global EIS and determining the information requirements of the system are the two main problems in the opinion of the respondents. This is consistent with the EIS literature findings (Young & Watson, 1995). It is important for developers to understand what is 'needed' by an executive and then develop a system that supports that need. An executives work environment encompasses a wide range of activities, which makes it difficult to develop a system that can adequately assist an executive. The fact that the users of the system include executives from different parts of the world makes the task of defining needs even more difficult. Getting executives to use the system was not considered to be a major problem. With the rapid advances in technology, executives will find it difficult to perform their jobs if they do not use technology. This might be a problem in subsidiaries located in certain parts of the world, as discussed earlier in the study. Determining the hardware and software required for the system and providing regional IT support in subsidiaries is not considered to be a problem in developing a global EIS.

CONCLUSION

This study reports and discusses the findings from 48 global companies, about the issues involved in developing, using, and managing a global executive information system. A summary of significant results is presented in the following paragraphs.

A global EIS should be global in scope, i.e., enterprise-wide and not regional or functional or based on one product division. Executive education in different parts of the world will impact the usage and diffusion of a global EIS in a global organization. The level and sophistication of the IT infrastructure available in subsidiaries of a global organization will impact the usage and success of the global EIS. Regulations on transborder data flows, acquisition of hardware and software, and usage of telecommunications equipment will have a impact on the usage/diffusion of a global EIS, though only moderate. The impact of using a global EIS, leading to a change in the distribution of power of members within an organization, is considered to be a moderately important issue. Economic factors, stability of national economies in subsidiaries and the currency restrictions imposed on the purchase of technological equipment are not considered to be of importance. A global EIS should have the capability of presenting data in multiple currencies, languages, and measurement units.

International business information used by a global EIS should be derived primarily from hard sources, for example, on-line databases, published information, academic institutions etc. The intensity of the global competition and the level of uncertainty that a company faces in its home country, i.e., the U.S., will create the need for additional sources of international business information. The usage of a global EIS by global organizations will lead to increased confidence in decision-making, increased organizational and individual learning and increased scanning of internal and external environments of a global company.

There is a strong support to include the CEO, and top management at headquarters and subsidiaries as primary users of a global EIS. Business executives at headquarters and subsidiaries should initiate the global EIS project. The global EIS project should be planned by a steering committee comprised of members from headquarters and subsidiaries. Asking executives directly is the recommended methodology for eliciting information requirements of executives. Prototyping and joint application development is recommended for developing the global EIS. A combination of in-house development and customization of off-the-shelf software is the recommended approach for developing a global EIS. A cross-cultural team comprising of 6–10 people should develop the global EIS. Business skills are considered the most important skills required of these people. The global EIS should be developed in a time-frame of 6–12 months. Top management should be actively involved in the development of the global EIS to ensure success of the system and adequate funding for the system.

A distributed configuration using an enterprise-wide network (WANs with workstations for interface) is the preferred hardware configuration for using a global EIS. On average, a global EIS costs $7.7 million approximately to develop and $784,423.08 to operate. The median cost to develop the system is $875,000 and the median operating cost is $147,500. The major component of this cost is software, followed by hardware and training.

Data integrity, security, and standards are considered to be important issues with respect to data management in a global EIS. Inclusion of a model management and knowledge management component in the global EIS will increase the quality of the system. Information should be presented in different formats (tabular, graphics, use of color etc.) for executives. E-mail and scheduler are desired features. The user-interface should be based on mouse/touch screen/menus and icons. All information should be provided on-line for executives.

Important reasons for developing a global EIS include: increases in quality of decision-making, usefulness for making strategic decisions, providing an organization with competitive advantages and providing access to unavailable information. Some of the problems for developing a global EIS include defining the objectives of the system, determining information requirements of the executives, and getting executives to use the system.

There were some surprises with respect to the global EIS study. The use of a global EIS will not lead to a decrease in the number of organizational levels involved in decision-making, a decrease in the involvement of subordinates required for analysis and a decrease in the frequency and duration of executive meetings. The use of a global EIS does not lead to faster task completion for an executive. There is not enough support to include middle management at headquarters or subsidiaries as primary users of the system. Respondents wanted all data to be processed at headquarters, rather than at regional or country processing centers. Determining hardware and software required for a global EIS and providing regional support in subsidiaries are not considered to be problems for the development and use of a global EIS.

EXPECTED CONTRIBUTIONS

This research study will contribute to the existing body of knowledge in several ways. This research study is perhaps the first attempt to address comprehensively the research questions listed earlier. Existing research has addressed the international dimension of functional areas (i.e. finance, marketing etc.) in organizations, but no previous comprehensive study exists in the area of global executive information systems. Further in the area of domestic EIS, practice led to research. Most of the publications are based on case studies or field surveys of actual systems being used by organizations. This study would enable the development of a systematic and cumulative body of knowledge for global EIS research. The global executive information systems research framework proposed in this study lays down the first step towards theory generation in the global EIS area. Identification of the key issues will assist researchers in conducting further research in the area. Academics can then build on the results of this study.

The proposed global EIS framework in the study would enable CIOs and other senior executives working in global organizations to better understand the issues that link the management of IS to the global environment. Watson et al. (1991) and Wetherbe (1991) point out that there are many instances of EIS failures in organizations. The framework proposed in this study and the results concerning issues that are important for management would ensure that mistakes are avoided in the development of a global EIS. The research question addressed in this research study should provide motivation for global organizations to develop and adopt a global EIS.

The study provides useful information for researchers and practitioners alike. At the same time it must be said that there are several questions that need to be examined further, especially because very little research has been conducted in this area. It would be interesting to conduct comparative studies of EISs developed and used in different parts of the world. Assessing benefits (quantifiable or tangible) of using a global EIS before the system is developed so that organizations may be able to perform cost/benefit analysis is another area which needs exploration. This may encourage more organizations to develop and use such systems.

The basis of a global EIS is the data that is processed for presentation to the executives. A detailed study of the data management problems for developing a global EIS is very important and should be explored in detail. How should a global EIS be integrated with other systems that an organization uses? What are some of the current technologies (e.g., Internet) that can be used for developing better quality global executive information systems? What would be some of the problems associated with processing data at regional and/or country centers rather than headquarters? How can these problems be overcome?

Bibliography

Armstrong, D.A. (1990, March 1). How Rockwell launched its EIS. *Datamation*.

Ball, D.A., & McCulloch, W.H. (1985). *International Business* (p. 11). Texas: Business Publications.

Barrow, C. (1990). Implementing an executive information system: Seven steps for success. *Journal of Information Systems Management*, 7(2), 41–46.

Bartlett, C.A., & Ghoshal, S. (1987). Managing across borders: New strategic requirements. *Sloan Management Review*, 28(4), 7–17.

Bartlett, C.A., & Ghoshal, S. (1989). *Managing across borders: The transnational solution*. Boston, MA: Harvard Business School Press.

Bartlett, C.A., & Ghoshal, S. (1992*). Transnational management:Text, cases and readings in cross-border management*. Homewood, IL: Irwin.

Benbasat, I., Goldstein, D.K., & Mead, M. (1987, September). The case research strategy in studies of information systems. *MIS Quarterly*, 369–386.

Berelson, B. (1952). *Content analysis in communication research*. Glencoe, IL: Free Press.

Bonoma, T.V. (1985a, May). Case research in marketing: Opportunities, problems, and a process. *Journal of Marketing Research*, 22, 199–208.

Bonoma, T.V. (1985b). *The Marketing Edge*. New York: Free Press.

Buss, M.D.J. (1982, September-October). Managing international information systems. *Harvard Business Review*, 153–162.

Carlyle, R. (1988, March 1). Managing IS at multinationals. *Datamation*, 54–57.

Carlyle, R. (1990, Feb. 1). The tomorrow organization. *Datamation*, 22–29.

Daft, R.L. (1992). *Organizational theory and design.* (p. 71). New York: West Publishing Company.

Davis, G.B., & Olson, M.H. (1985). *Management information systems: Conceptual foundations, structure and development.* (p. 215). McGraw-Hill Book Company.

Deans, P.C., & Kane, M.J. (1992). *International dimensions of information systems and technology.* Boston: PWS-Kent.

Deans, P.C., Karawan, K.R., Goslar, M.D., Ricks, D.A., & Toyne, B. (1991). Identification of the key international information systems issues in U.S. based multinational corporations. *Journal of Management Information Systems*, 7 (4), 27–50.

Deans, P.C., & Ricks, D.A. (1991). MIS research: A model for incorporating the international dimension. *The Journal of High Technology Management Research*, 2(1), 57–81.

Deans, P.C., & Ricks, D.A. (1993, Winter). An agenda for research linking information systems and international business: Theory, methodology and applications. *Journal of Global Information Management*, 1(1), 6–19.

DeLong, D.W., & Rockart, J.F. (1992). Identifying the attributes of successful executive support system implementation. In H.J. Watson, R. K. Rainer, & G. Houdeshel (Eds.), *Executive information systems: Emergence, development, impact* (pp. 257–277). New York: John Wiley & Sons, Inc.

Ein-Dor, P., & Segev, E. (1978). Organizational context and the success of management information systems. *Management Science*, 24, 1064–1077.

Eom, S.B. (1994, Spring). Transnational management strategies: An emerging tool for global strategic management. *SAM Advanced Management Journal*, 59(2), 22–27.

Egelhoff, W.G. (1993, Winter). Great strategy or great strategy implementation-two ways of competing in global markets. *Sloan Management Review*, 37–50.

Elam, J.J., & Leidner, D.G. (1995). EIS adoption, use, and impact: The executive perspective. *Decision Support Systems*, 14, 89–103.

Farrell, C., & Song, J. (1988, Winter). Strategic uses of information technology. *SAM Advanced Management Journal*, 10–16.

Freedman, D.H. (1985). Tying it together at the multinational. *Infosystems*, 32(2), 28–32.

Friend, D. (1990, March). EIS and the collapse of the information pyramid. *Information Center*, 6(3), 22–28.

Frolick, M., & Ramarapu, N.K. (1993, July). Hypermedia: The future of EIS. *Journal of Systems Management*.

Galbraith, J.R. (1977). *Organizational Design*. Reading, MA: Addison-Wesley Publishing Co.

Ghoshal, S. (1987) Global strategy: An organizing framework. *Strategic Management Journal*, 8, 425–440.

Ghoshal S., & Kim S.K. (1986, Fall). Building effective intelligence systems for competitive advantage. *Sloan Management Review*, 28 (1), 49–58.

Gorry, G.A., & Morton, M.S.S. (1989, Spring). A framework for management information systems. *Sloan Management Review*, 49–61.

Gummesson, E. (1991). Qualitative methods in management research. Sage Publications.

Hammer, M., and Mangurian, G.E. (1987, Winter). The changing value of communications technology. *Sloan Management Review*, 28(2), 65–71.

Hofstede, G. (1980). *Culture's consequences: International differences in work-related values*. Beverly Hills, CA: Sage.

Huff, S. L. (1991, Autumn). Managing global information technology. *Business Quarterly*, 56, 71–75.

Houdeshel, G., & Watson, H.J. (1987, March). The management information and decision support (MIDS) system at Lockheed-Georgia. *MIS Quarterly*, 11(1), 127–140.

Hout, T., Porter, M.E., & Rudden, E. (1982, September-October). How global companies win out. *Harvard Business Review*, 98–108.

Ives, B., Hamilton, S., & Davis, G.B. (1980, September). A framework for research in computer-based management information systems. *Management Science*, 26(9), 910–934.

Ives B., & Jarvenpaa S.L. (1991, March). Applications of global information technology:Key issues for management. *MIS Quarterly*, 15(1), 33–49.

Ives, B., & Learmonth, G.P. (1984). The information system as a competitive weapon. *Communications of the ACM*, 27(12), 1193–1201.

Ives B., Jarvenpaa S.L., & Mason R.O. (1993). Global business drivers: Aligning information technology to global business strategy. *IBM Systems Journal*, 32(1), 143–161.

Iyer, R.K. & Schkade, L.L. (1987). Management support systems for multinational business. *Information and Management*, 12, 59–64.

Johnson, H., & Vitale, M. (1988). Creating competitive advantage with interorganizational information systems. *MIS Quarterly*, 12(2), 153–165.

Jordan, E. (1993, August). Executive information systems for the chief information officer. *International Journal of Information Management*, 13(4), 249–259.

Kedia B.L., & Bhagat R.S. (1988). Cultural constraints on transfer of technology across nations: Implications for research in international and competitive management. *Academy of Management Review*, 13(4), 559–571.

Krippendorff, K. (1980). *Content analysis: An introduction to its methodology*. Newbury Park, CA: Sage.

Laudon, K.C., & Laudon, J.P. (1995). *Information systems: A problem-solving approach* (pp. 507–509). The Dryden Press.

Leidner, D.E., & Elam, J.J. (1993–1994, Winter). Executive information systems: Their impact on executive decision making. *Journal of Management Information Systems*, 10(3), 139–155.

Leidner, D.E., & Elam, J.J. (1994). Senior and middle management use of EIS: A descriptive study. *Proceedings of the Twenty-Seventh Annual Hawaii International Conference on Systems Sciences.*

Levitt, T. (1983, May-June). The globalization of markets. *Harvard Business Review*, 61(3), 92–102.

Mason, R.O., & Mitroff, I.I. (1973). A program for research on management information systems. *Management Science*, 19, 475–487.

Matthews, R., & Shoebridge, A. (1992, December). EIS-A guide for executives. *Long Range Planning*, 25(6), 94–101.

Meall, L. (1990, September). EIS: Sharpening the executive's competitive edge. *Accountancy*, 106(1165), 125–128.

Millet, I., & Mawhinney, C.H. (1992). Executive information systems: A critical perspective. *Information and Management*, 23, 83–92.

Min, H., & Eom, S.B. (1994). An integrated decision support system for global logistics. *International Journal of Physical Distribution and Logistics Management*, 24(1), 29–39.

Mintzberg, H. (1975, August). The manager's job: Folklore and fact. *Harvard Business Review*, 53(4), 49–61.

Moad, J. (1988, May 15). The latest challenge for IS is in the executive suite. *Datamation*, 43.

Moynihan, G.P. (1993, July). An executive information system: Planning for post-implementation at NASA. *Journal of Systems Management*, 44(7), 8–14.

Neo, B.S. (1991). Information technology and global competition. *Information and Management*, 20, 151–160.

Nolan, R.L., & Wetherbe, J.C. (1980, June). Towards a comprehensive framework for MIS research. *MIS Quarterly*, 1–19.

Nord, J.H. & Nord, G.D. (1995). Executive information systems: A study and comparative analysis. *Information and Management*, 29, 95–106.

Ohmae, K. (1990). *The borderless world*. New York: Harper Press.

Paller, A. (1990, January). *EIS conference report*, p. 4.

Palvia, S., Palvia, P., & Zigli, R.M., (Eds.). (1992). *The global issues of information technology management*. Harrisburg, PA: Idea Group Publishing.

Palvia, P., Kumar, A., Kumar, N., & Hendon, R. (1996). Information requirements of a global EIS: An exploratory macro assessment. *Decision Support Systems*, 16, 169–179.

Palvia, P.C., Palvia, S.C., & Roche, E.M., (Eds.). (1996). *Global information technology and systems management: Key issues and trends*. Nashua, NH: Ivy League Publishing, Limited.

Parsons G.L. (1983, Fall). Information technology: A new competitive weapon. *Sloan Management Review*, 1, 3–14.

Passino, Jr., J.H., & Severance, D.G. (1990, Spring). Harnessing the potential of information technology for support of the new global organization. *Human Resource Management*, 29(1), 69–76.

Perlmutter, H.V. (1969, January-February). The tortuous evolution of the multinational corporation. *Columbia Journal of World Business*, 9–18.

Porter M. & Miller V. (1985). How information gives you competitive advantage. *Harvard Business Review*, 62(4), 149–160.

Rainer,Jr., R.K., & Watson, H.J. (1995). What does it take for successful executive information systems? *Decision Support Systems*, 14, 147–156.

Reck, R.H. (1989, August 1). The shock of going global. *Datamation*, 67–69.

Roche, E.M. (1992). *Managing information technology in multinational corporations*. MacMillan Publishing Company.

Rockart, J.F., & DeLong, D.W. (1988*). Executive support systems: The emergence of top management computer use*. Homewood, IL: Dow Jones-Irwin.

Rockart, J.F., & Treacy, M.E. (1982, January-February). The CEO goes on-line. *Harvard Business Review*, 60(1), 81–93.

Rowe, A.J., Mason, R., & Dickel, K. (1986). *Strategic management: A methodological approach*. Reading, MA: Addison-Wesley.

Runge, L. (1988, June). On the executive's desk. *Information Center*,4(6), 34–38.

Sauter, V.L. (1992). Cross-cultural aspects of model management needs in a transnational decision support system. In Palvia, S., Palvia, P., & Zigli, R.M., (Eds.), *The global issues of information technology management* (pp. 332–355). Harrisburg, PA: Idea Publishing Group.

Simon, S.J. (1996). An informational perspective on the effectiveness of headquarters-subsidiary relationships: Issues of control and coordination. In P.C. Palvia,, S.C. Palvia, & E.M. Roche, (Eds.), *Global information technology and systems management: Key issues and trends* (pp. 249–275). Nashua, NH: Ivy League Publishing, Limited.

Sprague, R.H. Jr. (1980, December). A framework for the development of decision support systems. *MIS Quarterly*, 4(4).

Stecklow, S. (1989, April). The new executive information systems. Lotus, 51–53.

Toffler, Alvin (1991). *Powershift*. Bantam Doubleday Dell Publishing Group.

Turban, E. (1995). *Decision support and expert systems: Management support systems* (Rev. ed., pp. 400–440). Englewood Cliffs, NJ: Prentice Hall.

Violano, M. (1988, May). Friendly software for the bank CEO. *Bankers Monthly*, 105(5), 44–48.

Vitalari, N.P., & Wetherbe, J.C. (1996). Emerging best practices in global systems development. pp. 325–351. In P.C. Palvia, S.C. Palvia, & E.M. Roche, (Eds.). *Global information technology and systems management: Key issues and trends.* Nashua, NH: Ivy League Publishing, Limited.

Volonino, L., Watson, H.J., & Robinson, S. (1995). Using EIS to respond to dynamic business conditions. *Decision Support Systems*, 14, 105–116.

Waiter, J. (1995, July). Tomorrow is here. *Bobbin* , 36(11), 37–42+.

Watson, H.J. (1995, Spring). International aspects of executive information systems. *Journal of Global Information Management*, 3(2), 3.

Watson, H.J., Elam, J., Harris. J., Hertz, E., Rainer, R.K., Swift, R.S., Vogel, D.R. (1993). Panel: A research agenda for executive information systems. *Proceedings of the IEEE*, USA, 233–237.

Watson, H.J., & Frolick, M.N. (1992). Determining information requirements for an executive information system. In H.J. Watson, R. K. Rainer, & G. Houdeshel (Eds.), *Executive information systems: Emergence, development, impact* (pp. 161–175). New York: John Wiley & Sons, Inc.

Watson, H.J., Rainer Jr., R. K., & Koh, C.E. (1991, March). Executive information systems: A framework for development and a survey of current practices. *MIS Quarterly*, 13–30.

Wetherbe, J.C. (1991). Executive information requirements: Getting it right. *MIS Quarterly*, 51–65.

Wiseman, C. (1985). *Strategy and computers.* Homewood, IL: Dow Jones-Irwin, pp. 7.

Wiseman, C., & MacMillan, I. (1984, Fall). Creating competitive weapons from information systems. *Journal of Business Strategy*, 5, 42–49.

Yin, R.K. (1984). *Case study research.* Beverly Hills, CA: Sage Publications.

Yip, G.S. (1989). Global strategy . . . in a world of nations?. *Sloan Management Review*, 29–41.

Young, D., & Watson, H.J. (1995). Determinates of EIS acceptance. *Information and Management*, 29, 153–164.

Zmud, R.W. (1986). Supporting senior executives through decision support technologies: A review and directions for future research. In E.R. McLean & H.G. Sol (Eds.), *Decision support systems: A decade in perspective* (pp. 87–101). North-Holland, Amsterdam: Elsevier Science Publishers.

Index